To Bea Valiquette
Who in her quiet life of prayer
Became sacrament to each of us
May she rest in peace

Contents

Introduction:
Religious Experience

"Why do you weep when you pray?" he asked me, as though he had known me a long time.

"I don't know why," I answered, greatly disturbed.

The question had never entered my head. I wept because—because of something inside me that felt the need for tears. That was all I knew.

"Why do you pray?" he asked me, after a moment.

Why did I pray? A strange question. Why did I live? Why did I breathe?

"I don't know why," I said, even more disturbed and ill at ease. *"I don't know why."*

After that day I saw him often. He explained to me with great insistence that every question possessed a power that did not lie in the answer.

"Man raises himself toward God by the questions he asks Him," he was fond of repeating. . . . *"I pray to the God within me that He will give me the strength to ask Him the right questions."*[1]

1. Elie Wiesel, *Night,* trans. Stella Rodway (New York: Hill & Wang, Inc., 1960) 16.

These words help to frame the central thesis of this book. Why do we pray? What is it we do when we pray? Is prayer primarily for me, or for us, or for God? And is not the answer to these questions Yes? As we begin this book, our central concern is to get the questions right, to live with them, and to share with you our tentative answers.

On the wall of a cluttered office, a picture speaks to us. In a darkening shadow, a man holds a young girl on his shoulders and looks out at the ocean as the sun quietly sets beneath its floor. Written on the picture are the words: ''We ask God for answers, and He gives us a person to help us live with the questions.'' Prayer consists in getting the questions right and also in not having to ask them alone.

Within the Christian context, the person who helps us live with the questions is Jesus, the one who pitched his tent next to ours, who gives God a face, and who continues to ask us one question after another: Who do you say that I am? If I speak the truth, why do you strike me? Do you love me? Why have you forsaken me? But this enfleshed Jesus still lives among us, touches us in one another, prays in us, and shares our questions and our discoveries. We are a question-asking people. We struggle to ask our questions in the presence of our God and one another.

The central question of this small book asks: What is the relationship between our personal, individual prayer and the prayer we do with others in communal, liturgical prayer? We intend to focus on the often-missed similarities of these two ways of entering into our questing relationship with God, indicating that, though they are quite different modes of questing, both are primarily prayer.

For many Catholic Christians (and others, too), the liturgy, whether word, or sacrament, or both, has constituted the primary prayer. Often it has been the only form of prayer. We go to church on Sunday. Truly pious homes have often recited the rosary or read the Bible aloud, but for many, if not most, liturgical prayer was how and when we prayed. Some even went to Mass every day. Often this "Church" prayer has been ritualistic, even perfunctory. Our concern was to do it "right" (rubrically) more than to do it prayerfully, reflectively. Only in the past fifteen years have we begun to discover that liturgy can be personally involving, question-raising prayer.

Also, in recent years, average Christians have experienced an almost quantum leap of interest in the dimension of private, personal prayer, contemplation, and meditation. Many books on the theory and practice of prayer are published each year, all rushing to fill a void that has prevailed for decades. The popularity of Transcendental Meditation, the amazing growth of Zen and Yoga, the effectiveness of charismatic prayer groups, the revivification of retreat houses, and the rapid springing up of houses of prayer across the country: all are symptomatic of a new quest for personal integration of faith into life, moving our convictions from our heads to our hearts. Still the questions persist: Why do we pray? What do we do when we pray?

A recent study by Andrew Greeley reports that more than 85 percent of Americans will admit to having had some kind of religious experience, however they may couch that experience in words (experience of God, the awareness of transcendence, a union with the One, etc.). Frequently, almost universally, the reality of the person we name God crashes into people's lives or blows gently into the caves where they have hidden. Most of these experiences do not seem to effect much change or reach much depth. We simply have them, almost without noticing, then continue as we were before. There is little opportunity to discuss how the Lord has touched us as we watched a sunset, smelled a flower, or talked with a dying friend. The topic simply does not come up while we work on an assembly line at Boeing or play golf with friends.

We contend that the Lord touches people. We need to find ways to deepen that touch, to trust it, and to build our lives upon it. Prayer responds, then, to the questions: How do I remember, deepen, trust, and make operative my experiences of God? How do I do that in the quiet of my own unique heart? How do I bond together with others in ways that lessen my isolation and increase my trust in the touch that has occurred?

We need to make this more concrete. Consider three possibilities. I am driving across a floating bridge on a crisp spring day. The sun glistens on the water. The first sailboats slide along the water. I am instantly overwhelmed with a sense of being loved, a warmth, a well-being, and an unspoken, unspeakable conviction that there *is* a benignity beneath and beyond. I have not sought this flood of warmth, this touch of God, this faith-experience. It is a gift. I begin to relish it, just as a car swerves in front of me. I brake, honk, perhaps curse. The moment is over, but it need not be gone.

I am standing at the grave of a friend. The prayers are over. I wait a moment before entering again into the life from which my loved one has departed. As I look at the casket or the grave, a deep, unsought conviction settles over and within me. I *know* beyond the shadow of a doubt that my friend is alive. Resurrection is a fact, not a formulation of abstract faith. Tears well up, accompanied by embarrassment. I turn away, and return to life. I mention the experience to no one, and soon it disappears.

A friend is deeply troubled. She comes to me for advice or comfort. I am bewildered but compassionate. As I listen to her, I feel inadequate, uncertain how to respond. I have no words of my own. Something in me stirs, calling forth a word of challenge, even contradiction—a word foreign to my feelings and my ordinary way of relating. I am frightened by what I have just heard myself say, but my friend is startled, then moved, then crying, deeply grateful for what I have had the courage to say—just what she needed to hear. I do not know where the words came from, but I am aware of being gifted, graced, touched by God. The friend leaves. I begin to ponder the experience as the telephone rings. The moment and the experience disappear.

Myriad stories, as many as people to tell them, could flesh out these three examples. We do not know where or how God has touched you, only that he has done so. Our concern is that such moments not simply, silently, slip away. We need to relish them in quiet moments alone, and we need somehow to come together with others who, having felt similar moments, are not afraid to celebrate them. We all need to pray privately, in solitude, in order to relish, deepen, and come to trust the marvelous ways in which our God has loved us. We also need to render ourselves open to and available for further experiences. We all need to pray communally, liturgically, for exactly the same reasons. We also need to know that we are not alone, either in having or in trusting such experiences.

Our procedure will be to speak of personal, solitary prayer in three ways, indicating in each how liturgical prayer is similar. Prayer has to do with Life: our life, real life, the Life who is God. So does any liturgical, sacramental action of the Church. Prayer is an interpersonal response, a deepening of love relationships between persons: ourselves, God in Jesus Christ, and others. Liturgical prayer also, especially that prayer we call Eucharist, aims at deepening such interpersonal relationships in response to the source of life. Personal prayer, extended over any period of time, always becomes radical: it uproots and reroots us, transforms and recreates us in the image of Jesus. Liturgical prayer, especially that action of the Church called reconciliation, is also radically transforming.

Beneath each of the three areas lie the questions: Is not our personal prayer also in the deepest sense communal, affecting and affected by the prayer of others? And is not liturgical prayer also private and personal, deepening my unique, individual, progressively more radical response to life in and with Jesus?

Finally, as we begin, we invite you to bring your own very real experience with you. Before you move into the initial chapters, we invite you to close the book and remember. Remember the most significant graced moments of your life. Where has God been present to and alive in you? What moments, not necessarily in prayer, have moved you to believe deeply, even know? Were you on a mountaintop or sitting by a fire with a loved one? Did you hear a symphony or wait by the bedside as

13

a dear one died? Has there been a time when the priest held up the sacred host and said, "This *is* the Lamb of God," and it *was,* and you knew it? Is there a forgotten moment when you experienced not just the words of absolution but also a deep sense of being loved and forgiven despite your failures and inadequacies? What have been your experiences of God? Have you trusted in them and let them direct your life in any way? Have you treasured these graced moments in your heart? Have you in any way built your life upon them?

Perhaps an exercise will help you enter into these reflections. Draw a line, graphing the story of your life. Begin at birth and end at the present. Draw high points and low points. Remember the people, places, and events that moved you here or there. Take time. Look at the graph as your own personal Exodus experience. God leads you from slavery to freedom. How has he done this? How have you responded?

Be quiet, grateful, hopeful.

What next?

1

Personal Prayer and Life

> *"They have taken my Lord away,"* she re-
> *plied, "and I don't know where they have put*
> *him."* As she said this she turned round and
> *saw Jesus standing there, though she did not*
> *recognize him.*

John 20:13–14

Prayer is the discovery of Jesus within the fabric of our lives. The resurrection accounts in each Gospel help us to appreciate this. In prayer we relate to the risen Jesus. In many ways we meet him now as they met him then, in the events of life.

Mary, discouraged and depressed after the burial of one who had loved her into life, searches frantically for the missing body. Her inner turmoil is so intense that she is not aware of things and persons around her. She pays little attention to the gardener and so at first does not recognize the Lord, who comes to her, until he speaks her name: "Mary." Only then does she recognize the presence already at hand, presence that had been there as she searched.

The apostles, despondent and uncertain after the death of Jesus, go back to their familiar pursuits, go fishing in their familiar boats. They catch nothing, working futilely. A stranger on the shore calls to them, cooks for them. Only with a careful, second look does John realize "it is the Lord." He was where they were all along.

The road back to Emmaus from Jerusalem seemed long and lonely to the followers of Jesus. They heard rumors of his presence but doubted them. They were unable to look carefully outside themselves at the traveler who joined them on the road. Even as he spoke to them, they avoided awareness of their burning hearts, till finally they knew him in the breaking of the bread, though he had been there all along, talking of their lives, hopes, dashed dreams. And when recognized, then as now, he quickly vanished, and they had to return to other believers in order to trust in what they had experienced.

The stories still are true. While we frantically search for Jesus in all the wrong places, he walks beside us, works in a garden, prepares an unexpected meal, or pushes a shopping cart next to ours in a supermarket.

Our personal experience constitutes the starting point of prayer. If we look for God aside from that, we look in vain. The story is told that the Russian cosmonaut Yuri Gagarin returned from a space flight and reported caustically that he had not seen God. A Russian Orthodox priest replied, "If you have not seen him on earth, you will never see him in the heavens."

In our book *Inviting the Mystic, Supporting the Prophet* (Paulist, 1981), we suggest that personal prayer is not so much something we do as a response to and an immersion in our experience—a growing awareness of love and forgiveness, the painful loss or forming of relationships, sickness or the vitality of health, celebration or mourning. We must see our experience as more than a series of events or persons, however. It is rather a process in which God transforms us through our very living and being. Prayer is really a way of *be*-ing before God, before all that is. The more we are open to the truth and goodness of everything and everyone that exists, the more we are truly at prayer.

The world is sacramental

Life and prayer are not separate or separable. We live here. We pray there. Just as everything is prayer, so everything is (or can be) sacramental, a thing made holy. Jesus—Alpha and Omega; beginning, end, and middle; totally present—pervades our reality. "There lives a dearest freshness, deep down things," as "Christ plays in ten thousand places." The Lord can touch us anywhere, anytime. In the Northwest of these United States, Mount Rainier stands as a constant symbol of God —majesty, beauty, power, awe, often even a matter of faith because it is invisible behind clouds or rain. Anyone who lives in this area can be led to God through that marvelous, mysterious mountain. The same is true of the waters of Puget Sound or Lake Washington, or the colors of autumn, or the smell of spring. We can be in the presence of the holy—graced, gifted, aware of God's love—as we sit before a fireplace and listen to Beethoven, Bach, or Bartok; as we walk hand-in-hand with a friend; as we are overcome by the stars of night or the sunshine of a glorious day. A sailboat, a coffin, a flower, a beer—anything can be sacred, a sign of God's graciousness flowing into us as part of the gift of life.

My life

Prayer must be rooted in my life, not John of the Cross's, Teresa of Avila's, a friend's, or my husband's or wife's. We all have a tendency to look at others and assume that their prayer is wonderful. We become depressed with our own by comparison. But this futile waste of energy and time ignores the deep and wonderful reality that our relationship with the Lord is unique, and so is our prayer.

How often a husband is discouraged by his inability to be as quiet as his wife, as attentive and still and apparently ready, listening. He is sure he does not pray because he does not pray as she does. One day she asks him what he thinks about as he works on the car on a Saturday afternoon. After a moment he responds, a little shyly, how that day he found himself overwhelmed by the complexity of the car, how he found God's enormous ability to love the complexity of our world. He noticed the interconnectedness of things in the car and in the world. He saw the lines that carried power throughout the automobile as God's graciousness flowing through our veins, our limbs, our hearts. He had never spoken to her like that before. She had thought he never prayed, and so had he. They discover, wonderfully, that they simply pray differently; God touches them in different ways.

Life as it is

Prayer flows out of my life as it is, not as I think it should be. As I visit my closest friend, I spill out my deepest desires, blackest fears, strongest hopes. I would not think of engaging in some sort of stereotypical, formalized conversation with a dear friend. Why should it be different with the Lord? If I am angry, I bring that anger to my prayer to be accepted and sorted out. I might be angry with God. If I am lonely or depressed, I bring those feelings before God. I do not pretend to be other than I am.

We have a friend, a rather ordinary-looking priest. He often speaks of how he enters into prayer with the words: "Well, Lord, here's good old sexy George!"

Tevye in *Fiddler on the Roof* always prays from where he really is in simple, direct, honest intouchness with his life and with his God: "Lord, I know we are the chosen people, but sometimes you couldn't choose somebody else?"

How often we have mumbled the well-worn formula: "O my God, I am heartily sorry for having offended thee, and I detest all my sins because of thy just punishments. . . ." What I really want to say is: "I am not very sorry for my sins; in fact, I am rather fond of them, attached to them. I am not afraid of hell because I know you love me, but I would like to be different than I am." The point is, we need to be honest before God with what is truly occurring in our life.

Certainly we need to spend time in personal prayer, in solitude, and not just hope to see God everywhere in everything. Without giving adequate quiet-time to prayer, we will not easily discover God's presence flowing through our lives. But some would *limit* prayer to periods of solitude, as if that were our only prayer. Henri Nouwen touches on this in his book *Intimacy* when he mentions a friend with such a mindset. After many disrupted prayer periods, his friend finally realized that the myriad, frustrating interruptions throughout his carefully planned day were more truly the substance of his prayer. He recognized the need of being open to and welcoming of the Christ who came with others into the corners of his life.

Life in relationship to others

Personal prayer must never be insulated from the lives of others. To pray to the God who is present everywhere, and yet to ignore his presence in the homeless, the dispossessed, the marginal people of all types, is to violate the most basic assumption about prayer. My prayer is authentic insofar as I allow the life and death of others to impinge on it. Sometimes we mistakenly think that thoughts of ''the world'' are distractions in our prayer rather than the agenda God provides. God often seems to want our focus not upon himself but upon the ones he specially loves.

Archbishop Raymond Hunthausen of Seattle is remarkably prayerful. One cannot be in his presence and not sense his openness to the Spirit of God, the power of Jesus. He also finds at times that he must, out of that prayer, be outspoken as a leader in the world. Precisely because he prays, he cannot ignore the presence of a nuclear submarine base or the MX missile plant in the very heart of his diocese. These realities deeply affect the lives of others, and hence they are part and parcel of his life, his prayer.

Eternal life

Prayer is not only a response to life. It is also an opening of oneself to the gift of eternal life, the gift by which we live as sons and daughters of our

Father-Mother God and can cry out "Abba." The life that the Father gives us is the life of his Son, Jesus Christ, given through the power of the Holy Spirit. The gift of the life of the Father and the Son *is* the Holy Spirit. We who possess the Spirit possess everything that belongs to the Father and the Son (John 14–17).

The intimate relationship between prayer and life is lost when we forget the Holy Spirit. The biblical terms for Spirit (Hebrew: *ruah,* Greek: *pneuma)* denote movement of air, wind, breath, and life. As Paul says, "The Spirit gives life" (2 Cor 3:6). It is the Spirit that gifts us with life, with prayer.

The life of prayer is a life guided by Christ's own, as Paul repeatedly tells us (Rom 8:15, 26–27; Gal 4:6–7). The Spirit bearing witness with our spirit allows us to be caught up into Jesus' own movement to the Father and, therefore, into his own life of prayer.

This sounds extremely abstract until we reflect on our own prayer-experience, spontaneously aware of the name of a friend or the hurt of a loved one without consciously calling either to mind or heart. Sometimes we have found a word of Jesus to be our word as we call out "Abba" or "Be it done according to your will." The Spirit speaks in us. In *We Cannot Find Words* (Denville, N.J.: Dimension Books, 1981, 6), Tad Dunne calls human consciousness the "bursting-out place for God's spirit within the womb of Creation."

To learn to pray is to learn to allow the prayer of Jesus to well up within us. The ancient phrase "to place ourselves in the presence of God" means simply to become aware of Christ, who prays constantly. In effect, we pray because we have arrived; we act because the action is already going on. The risen Christ, whom we perhaps only dimly recognize, lives and prays constantly in us. We sum this up each time we celebrate the Eucharist when we affirm:

> Through him, with him, in him,
> in the unity of the Holy Spirit,
> all glory and honor is yours,
> almighty Father, for ever and ever. Amen.

Sharing the life

A sense of bondedness with all persons flows from the realization that Jesus lives and prays in each of us through the power of the Spirit. My prayer, my life, is linked with the life and prayer of others. My life of prayer, even in solitude with the Lord, is always "shared" prayer since the power that allows that prayer and flows from it is not mine but a power shared with every prayer and every praying person.

One may ask: If all this is true, why is my prayer so dry, so halfhearted, and so miserable most of the time? Our response relates to the tension between the already-accomplished and the not-yetness of our lives. A Christian is always one who is redeemed by Christ, yet one who still runs the race (Phil 3:12), still struggles to accept that gift, still experiences that sense of being a pilgrim on the way. This tension is manifest in the way the power of the Spirit comes and goes in our prayer. It reminds us that prayer is a free gift, a power we do not possess in and of ourselves.

We may also labor under the hidden assumption that what is unsatisfying or boring to us is also unsatisfying or boring to God. We forget that the journey to God is always and everywhere one of faith—a faith that believes God's power is present, a power that continues to be operative even when its presence is not felt. Especially at such times do we need to look at the rest of our life for authentication of God's living power at work in us. We cannot judge the effectiveness of our prayer by how we feel while we are praying in solitude but only by how well we love when we are living among others. As we become increasingly more loving, more a sacrament of God's presence to others, we need not fear. All the great mystics point out that the deepest growth in our life in the Spirit usually comes to us precisely in the darkness of faith as we grow in Christian love.

Finally, in terms of prayer that grows out of life —our unique, individual life—it is unfortunate that the term *imitation of Christ* has become so descriptive of interior spirituality and is so often applied to our life of prayer. What we seek is not simply a deeper imitation of Jesus but rather to be animated (inspired) by the Spirit of the risen Christ, who lives and prays within us now, who chooses to touch others through us. To pray is to choose life— my life—in union with the life of the risen Lord. To pray is to be ever more immersed in all of life and to be blessed and enriched and graced because of that immersion.

Everything we have said about prayer thus far— that it is about life and not simply the saying of prayers—is aptly summarized by Thomas Merton:

> It's a risky thing to pray, and the danger is that our very prayers get between us and God. The great thing in prayer is not to pray but to go directly to God. If saying your prayers is an obstacle to prayer, cut it out. Let Jesus pray. Thank God Jesus is praying. Forget yourself. Enter into the prayer of Jesus. Let him pray in you. The best way to pray is: stop. Let prayer pray within you, whether you know it or not. This means a deep awareness of our true inner identity. . . . But the point is that we need not justify ourselves. By grace, we are Christ. Our relationship with God is that of Christ to the Father in the Holy Spirit.[1]

1. Quoted by David Steindl-Rast, *Thomas Merton, Monk: A Monastic Tribute,* ed. Patrick Hart (New York: Sheed and Ward, Inc., 1974) 87–88.

2

The Sacraments
as Prayer of Life

*I have come
so that they may have life
and have it to the full.*

John 10:10

Everything said about prayer in the previous chapter also applies to liturgical, sacramental, communal prayer. Liturgy relates to life: our life, my life. As with any prayer, it leads to life and flows from life. Everything in this chapter aims to support this simple realization.

In the last fifteen years every liturgical action of the Church has exemplified dramatic change. We Catholics perceive the changes within the Liturgy of the Eucharist (spoken in English, facing the people, fuller participation, sharing in the cup, wider range of and diversity in the readings, etc.). We are less aware that similar changes have occurred within each of the other sacramental celebrations of our Church. Baptism now focuses on the parents instead of the child and is often celebrated at Sunday Eucharist. Confirmation emphasizes mission in the Spirit rather than reception of the Spirit, and it climaxes not in a slap by the bishop but in the ancient imposition of hands. Reconciliation is often celebrated within a communal setting, or individually face-to-face. And thus with every other sacramental action.

Most changes heighten our realization of sacraments as prayer, prayer of a community, prayer that touches on the life of that community responding to the questions: Where are we, who are we, and how are we together before God? In each case, the change in liturgical ritual grows out of a significant change in the theology of the sacrament being celebrated.

In the following pages we offer reflections on how and why the liturgical celebration of our sacramental life in the Church has changed. Throughout, a unifying element remains—we speak of prayer, of how we enter into the mystery of God's love for us, and of how we celebrate and deepen that love.

Sacraments give grace

In almost any gathering of Catholic Christians, the question "Why do we receive the sacraments?" receives the answer "To get grace!" That answer, though true, invites massive misunderstanding. We suggest half-seriously that the word *grace* be dropped from our vocabulary for the next fifty years until it recovers its rich original meaning.

What does the word *grace* mean?

Though it appears flippant and irreverent to suggest it, most of us grew up with a notion of grace as a very "thingy" thing indeed. Born into life with an empty bucket (not graced), we traveled through life doing things that "earned" grace. We gradually filled our bucket, careful to refrain from those things through which grace could leak out or (horrors!) pour out of the bucket. If we had enough grace in our personal bucket when we died, we would get into heaven. If we did not have quite enough grace, we would earn a temporary and relieved purgatory. If there were no grace at all, our empty bucket would merit eternal weeping and gnashing of teeth in an exterior darkness. Most of us were weaned on catechism books with a picture of a large cloud labelled "grace" from which seven rays of light streamed down upon an individual underneath. The religious task seemed to consist in knowing when to draw the grace we needed from the appropriate spring.

Our God, however, is not a thing. We are not things. Grace is not a thing. Our God is personal. A far more compelling and precise understanding would picture two people stretching their arms out toward one another, giving and receiving love.

The word *grace* has the same root as *gracious, gratuitous,* meaning "freely given," "unearned." The notion of earning grace is internally contradictory, heretical, Pelagian. We cannot merit God's love. Moreover, the *grace,* the *unearned gift* of God, is not a thing but the person Jesus Christ. To receive *grace* is to enter initially or more deeply into a relationship of love with Jesus. When Paul says, "I live now not with my own life but with the life of Christ who lives in me" (Gal 2:20), he describes what we have come to call *grace.* Mary is blessed, "full of grace," because the presence of Jesus has taken flesh in her womb.

In liturgical, sacramental celebration we receive grace insofar as we receive the gift of God in Jesus Christ. This reception, neither magic nor automatic, requires only presence on our part, honest receptivity to the growth of that relationship.

Most of us have ridden on a bus, perhaps the same one, for many days or weeks. Some time later we attend a wedding reception or go to a party and see someone who looks familiar to us. After a few moments of conversation, we realize that both of us had been riding that same bus together every morning. We never met. No relationship began. Perhaps the seed of friendship had been planted and will begin to take root now, but we had not been graced (gifted) with friendship in that frequent proximity. She had been on the bus, I had been on the bus, but we had never met. Sacraments have often been like that. Jesus was there, we were there, but we never met—never really touched and began a life of intimacy together. We went to church, went through a ritual, but did not experience the graciousness. Love did not begin, or grow, or deepen.

When we say "sacraments give grace," we had best say "maybe." If they become prayer. If our lives intermingle with the life of Jesus. If we meet and are touched and loved more fully to life.

Jesus Christ, the sacrament of God

There is only one sacrament: Jesus, the sacrament of God, the one made holy, sacred. As in every love relationship, we may experience the beloved in a variety of ways, but it is still the same person we meet. We may meet a friend at one time. Initially, after some central decision to build a relationship, we confirm ourselves in that direction. We find union between us as our lives, our stories, interweave and overlap. At times we need to apologize or forgive, or the relationship will die. In these and many other ways, friendship grows and flourishes, but it remains one and the same friendship. The seven sacraments are a diversity of prayer experiences in which we meet and grow in intimacy with the same person, Jesus, in a variety of ways.

The Church, the body of Christ, is—or ought to be—the sacrament, the sacred sign, the thing made holy. In and through and with the People of God, the community of believers who profess the same conviction that Jesus is the Lord, we encounter and deepen our relationship with that Lord. The

31

Church comprises not merely people who *receive* sacraments but also people who *become* sacraments, sacred signs, vehicles for God's love to the Church itself and to the world. We do not simply get baptized into Christ's life, death, and resurrection. We are welcomed into an entire community of people building their lives on that belief. We find Christ not only in a tiny piece of bread designated "the body of Christ" but in a people designated the same way because they share that meal. We come to know how faithful the love of Jesus is when we see communities of married couples mirror that fidelity in their sacramental covenant. There is only one sacrament: Jesus Christ. The Church, a community of believers, is the place of meeting with that one sacrament in a variety of ways.

The sacraments do not save us

The sacraments do not magically save us. They are not rituals that somehow win God's approval and become the means of our salvation. They are not actions to be performed correctly, not things to be done, not hoops to be jumped through in order to win, or even receive, God's love. Paschal is reported to have said, only slightly in jest, that sacraments were things that Catholics did to avoid the awesome task of trying to love each other. Receiving sacraments does not constitute us as good ("He's a good Catholic; he always goes to church."), holy, redeemable, or redeemed. Faith in Jesus Christ saves us. To the extent that we already believe that we are saved, Jesus has shown God's love to us. As we meet Jesus over and over again in sacramental prayer, we deepen and express the union that has already occurred.

Let us be more concrete. We are already children of God. God is father-mother-creator of all and so lies at the source, the base, the root, of our lives. Baptism does not make God accept someone that God would otherwise not have liked. Baptism does not make one a child of God. Baptism *celebrates* and *deepens,* acknowledges and brings to consciousness, what already was true. It is a prayer that commits us to live with more awareness of the reality that already pervades our lives—our deep, personal relationship with a loving God. To the extent that baptism is prayer, related to our very real lives, it becomes a means by which a child and, more important, the child's parents and the entire supporting community become more deeply aware of the preciousness of life, of the possibility of community, of the eternally loving relationship with God—one they promise to share with that emerging person.

Similarly, the sacrament of reconciliation (penance, confession) does not create or cause God's forgiveness, though we have often talked as if it did. God's forgiveness is not dependent on the precise performance of a particular ritual. That forgiveness is always ours, always available, always ready to touch us. In fact, if we did not already know that God forgives, we would not be likely to celebrate the sacrament. The sacrament does acknowledge this forgiveness, does prayerfully celebrate it, and does, we hope, deepen our individual and collective awareness of God's mercy. The son would never have climbed out of the pig-sty to return to the father's house if he had not known already how gentle and forgiving his father could be. The sacrament does not cause God's forgiveness.

Certainly, when our lives are ended, the question will not be whether we received sacraments but whether we accepted them—became them—because Jesus had been transforming our lives with his own.

Sacraments heighten the all-pervasiave reality of God's presence

In the previous chapter we spoke of God totally present in our lives and our experiences. The whole world is sacramental, or can become so to the eyes of a believer. Just as everything can be prayer, so everything can be a channel of grace, that is, a means to meeting Jesus. The Church, recognizing this, celebrates seven key moments of human life to help us realize more fully this constant fact. Again, sacraments are prayer, prayer related to life. If they are not woven into and drawn out of the fabric of our lives, sacraments remain empty rituals.

34

Concretely, if the Eucharist is effective, every meal shared with friends becomes more and more a cause of thanksgiving. Reconciliation, prayerfully experienced, fosters constant human forgiveness and becomes a consistent reminder of a God who loves us no matter what we do. If a marriage is truly sacramental, the couple's fidelity inspires themselves and everyone whose life they touch. If we are authentically baptized into the community of God's family, and if we truly do welcome a new member into the body of Christ, then all our communities, families, even clubs and teams, become welcoming, open, and receptive gatherings of people. Sacraments are effective (efficacious) to the extent that they open our eyes to the sacramental reality of God's love everywhere.

Each sacrament focuses on a significant dimension of all life

Each of the seven sacraments celebrated liturgically within the Church relates closely to the challenge of human beings to be fully alive in Christ, who comes that we may have abundant life. Each is prayer intimately connected with life. In crisis time, in key moments of personal and communal history, sacraments celebrate stages of special importance in the Easter-life of Jesus as these stages are mirrored in individual persons and communities. Each sacrament is, quite literally, a matter of life and death in which we adamantly, over and over again, choose life. "I set before you life or death . . . . Choose life" (Deut 30:19). And we do. Each time we prayerfully celebrate a sacrament of the Church, we re-enter the covenant relationship with our God. Let us briefly touch upon this covenant dimension as it is signified in each sacrament. These hints can be developed as we begin to capture more concretely how sacraments and life, sacraments and prayer, are inextricably related.

Baptism

At birth a human being is fragile. Only others can save the child from death—personal, psychological, spiritual, social, economic. The Christian community does not deny that all these demonic forces exist, does not deny the possibility of death in many forms. Rather, we affirm Jesus Christ as a force for life that overcomes death in all its forms. With infant baptism, the community commits itself to fostering life in this child, to helping this child withstand the forces of death. The child begins to meet Christ in a community that wants to pledge itself to be and to become a life-giving part of that child's existence.

We remain with baptism for a moment to see how it needs to be prayerfully related to life in order to be authentic. (We will not pursue this explication with each sacrament, but the obvious implications can be drawn for each.) We cannot celebrate any sacrament the same way every time, in every place, in every community. We often hear people remark how differently they celebrate Mass in *that* church. They must, precisely because *that* church is not *this* church, and over there is not here. Each community needs to make each sacrament reflective of its own unique life. Baptism cannot be exactly the same ceremony for every culture, nor for every child within a given culture.

Concretely, the baptismal rite contains a moment in which we verbally say no to evil, yes to God in Jesus. We "renounce Satan, and all his works, and all his empty promises." We affirm God, Jesus, the Spirit, the Church, eternal life. We say no to sin, yes to love. We proclaim our readiness to die, to enter into the waters, to be buried in them, to put to death an old destructive way of seeing, being, and believing, so that we may rise out of the waters to new life with Jesus. Thus, we baptize into death so that we can rise to new life. In infant baptism we affirm life and reject death on behalf of an infant. We pledge ourselves to a value system, a vision of life over and against death-forces that could otherwise kill this human spirit bursting into life.

This vision has serious implications for the celebration of the rite. It must necessarily vary from culture to culture, family to family. Baptism cannot be the same in every instance because the forces of death and the means to life vary enormously. In some cultures—in Africa or Latin America, for example—the forces of death may be found in the difficulty of achieving an education or in the likelihood of accepting second-class citizenship and bare subsistence. Some children may be threatened with the death that results from cultural oppression because they happen to be black or female. In another culture, the satanic (demonic) that needs to be renounced may be the constant competitive temptation to be "Number One," or the inclination of an affluent society to waste and take for granted the limited goods of the earth.

The members of a community celebrating baptism or any other sacrament need to take time to reflect on what their prayer, their hope, and their promise properly are. They need to consider what it means in their lives today, how God wants to love them as they are and not as they would like (or pretend) to be.

Confirmation

Generally we still celebrate confirmation as a separate sacrament, a delayed part of initiation into the Christian community. We wait sometimes until late adolescence or early adulthood. As a community, we deal with life-or-death questions that now may be owned by the individual as his or her own. A child grows under the guidance of the community, increasingly aware of the reality and the power of Jesus in human life. The child has begun to realize the life-giving effect of the message and meaning of Jesus. As the person moves into adulthood, he or she makes the choice personally. Will she choose life? Will he choose to use his liberty for the good of this community and the human family? Will she be able to sort her way through the destructive forces that surround and threaten her? Will he be able to sustain and foster hope?

As the individual Christian totters on the edge of adulthood, the Christian community gathers again to celebrate the anointing of someone who is loved not just as a survivor but as a victor. The individual meets Christ again within this community and pledges to join the others in the struggle to liberate themselves and the world. "To become a soldier of Christ," as our ancient understanding would have it, means more precisely to join with others in the struggle of Jesus to build the Father's kingdom of justice, love, and peace. We confirm the individual in that commitment as the community not only pledges support but also accepts the promise to be supported by this new and now fully initiated Christian.

Eucharist

We will return to this sacrament later and at length. Here we would only point out that this sacrament constitutes not a "moment" in our history but a continually enduring reality. The communion question persists: Is permanence and solidity possible in human community?

We are constantly tempted to deny this possibility. "How easily things get broken," Leonard Bernstein writes. "Things fall apart, the center cannot hold," laments Yeats. We are rendered dead by routine. Over and over again, we celebrate this prayerful sign that we *are* one, that communitarian love is possible, that we can be and are knit together in love because the life of Jesus flows through the veins and enlivens the flesh of us all. Communion constantly and prayerfully confirms the hope and expectation that we can remain one with Jesus and with each other. We will not die nor let others die.

Reconciliation

Intimately connected with the hope of communion is the antithetical moment of rupture. We will return also to this reconciling moment again and at length. Here we wish only to point out the constant reality of breaking from a community no matter how often or how well our communion is signed, sacramentalized, prayed. All sin is anticommunitarian. We continually face the life-question: Is it possible to refashion love that has been undone?

Though humanly tempted to say no, the Christian community answers by celebrating Christ's pardon and by continually reaccepting us into the community against which we have sinned. We admit, celebrate, and are challenged by our proclamation, with Jesus, that no love progresses without death and resurrection, without sin and re-integration.

Marriage

The community celebrates with two people who proclaim the truth that deep, lasting love, mirroring God's love for his people, endures despite all the forces of death that deny or try to kill it. They will be signs to each other of a love that persists in good times and bad, sickness and health, all the days of their lives.

Priesthood

To what extent can we burn our bridges in love? The priest is anointed, called by God and the community to love and serve without stint. Death and resurrection are signified by ordaining a person's love for the community. The community celebrates the possibility of life lived in service of others.

Anointing of the sick

Imminent death provides an obvious moment of crisis, especially because at that moment we cannot help asking what the passive, suffering person can do that indicates life. The community comes together again to celebrate, signify, sacramentalize, and prayerfully assert that the sick person is still loved, still important. We affirm that we want our beloved back, whole and healthy among us, if possible. If not, we celebrate the way in which the person is here and now positively constructing the final definitive living body of Christ with which we shall all be joined in life forever. Even at the moment of death, we affirm life.

All of the above are simply hints at the depth hidden in the community's prayerful celebration of each sacrament. Each could be extended and magnified. The connection between each sacrament and the larger sacramental world could be pointed out. Our concern is that liturgy be prayer, that sacraments be prayerful realizations of our role as individuals and communities struggling with the realities of life.

Two final reflections seem necessary.

Sacraments are for the world

The whole sacramental reality, the whole prayer of which we have been speaking, exists not just for the Church, not just for believers, but for the entire world. Sacraments provide the leaven in the dough that makes the whole thing rise. Each Christian community celebration proclaims what God has done within this community and also challenges this community regarding what it has done for the world. How have we furthered God's saving work? A Eucharist that does not challenge us to be more deeply in union with all people and help us to unite with one another is a false Eucharist, mere ritual. In fact, each Eucharist either reaffirms the status quo or challenges us to move in new ways. Reconciliation that does not call us to heal a wounded world is empty form. The forgiven servant must in turn forgive the debts of others. And thus with each of the sacraments. This point will be developed further when we speak of prayer as radical, in the context of the specific sacrament of reconciliation.

Sacraments are vocations

Every sacrament, every moment in liturgical prayer, is a beginning of life in the Lord Jesus, not an ending, the first and not the final act. In a real sense, we are not baptized when we go through the sacramental act, but we begin to be baptized. We are called (vocationed) to live not for ourselves but in Jesus. We do not yet do that perfectly. We have not totally put on Christ at the moment of baptism but have committed ourselves (or been committed) to do so. No child is perfect immediately after baptism. We who are already baptized are too obviously inclined to some envy, pettiness, or selfishness. We have not finished the work at baptism but have merely begun it.

The married couple leaving the church after the ceremony are not yet two in one flesh, but they are called, within that sacrament, to become so. They are not yet signs of God's faithful love for each other and for the community, but they have accepted a call to try to become that. It will take years before they look the same, laugh at the same things, finish each other's sentences, and amaze us by their oneness. The prayer of the sacrament is that they be enabled and empowered to do so. It starts now, not finishes.

In all of the above we are asserting that prayer is about life. Sacraments are prayer and thus are involved in life. Liturgy, too, is prayer which must have to do with life, create life, celebrate life, deepen life. All our rituals have been changed in the past few years to help that happen.

3

Personal Prayer as Response

I tell you most solemnly, if you do not eat the
flesh of the Son of Man and drink his blood,
you will not have life in you. All who do eat
my flesh and drink my blood have eternal life,
and I shall raise them up on the last day. For
my flesh is real food and my blood is real
drink. All who eat my flesh and drink my
blood live in me and I live in them.

John 6:53–56

Solitary prayer is a personal response within a relationship. In prayer we enter into the fullest, most
integrating, most demanding, most life-giving relationship possible. There is only one relationship,
an interpersonal growth in and with God in Jesus
Christ that can fulfill, integrate, and center our
lives.

There are other relationships at every level of
our lives that can seduce and entrap us, seeming to
be more fulfilling and ultimate. Before we reflect
on the response that is prayer, we need to examine
our response within these other relationships that

also involves our development, our search for meaning, our longing for fulfillment.

Relationship with oneself

We do each have a relationship with ourselves. At times this seems like all we have, and most human beings experience the desire, at times, to be a rock, an island—touching no one, with no one touching them.

Things and other people can disappoint us so badly that we are tempted to rely on ourselves, and only ourselves. We will stand alone, do our job, fulfill our duties, and then, like the Lone Ranger, ride off into the sunset, untouched by the people or events surrounding us. We are afraid, protective, controlled, alone.

The novels of Ayn Rand appeal to the college student searching for independence from family, religion, and culture, hoping to make it "by myself" and "on my own." The inexperienced can easily be drawn to a stance of rugged individualism and hope for the fulfillment of Sysiphus—it may not mean anything that I push this rock up this hill and have done it a thousand meaningless times, but "By God, I did not quit." "I did it my way," as the song says.

Even blessed with a healthy self-image, we move into adulthood and soon realize that we cannot find the meaning of our lives in our self. Most of us are only too aware of the ambiguity, tension, and division within that breeds despair and depression. Relating only to ourselves in isolation from honest interaction with others and the external world around us, we go mad. We may survive, may avoid some pain, may even reach a modicum of external success, but we will not be fulfilled as human beings when we focus on ourselves, for ourselves, by ourselves. We need to be related outward.

Relationship with things

We live constantly in relationship with things. The immediately seductive temptation is to believe that we can be humanly fulfilled in relationship to the materiality of our world. Commercials constantly bombard us with the expectation that this car, house, boat, bank account, scotch, toothpaste, or Band-Aid will make all the difference. Caught up in this futile search, wounded people all around have discovered that each acquisition creates the taste for another. If one boat is good, two will be better. The search never ends, never fulfills, never satisfies. Most of us soon recognize the futility of satisfaction through things.

A more subtle form of the seductive power of things is evident in our desire for success, our anxiety to please significant others, or our search for the bauble reputation. We expect to be fulfilled by intellectual achievement, a degree attained, a book published, or by excellent physical health, the perfect figure or physique. These also tempt us and, though good in themselves, never satisfy the longing to be whole, complete, integrated.

Often it is the good things, the best things, that are most seductive. We can make idols out of a religious community, the Church, liberation movements, a position we hold, or a service we perform. James Fowler speaks of this as henotheism, attributing ultimate concern to that which is less than ultimate worth. We worship at an altar on which sits the faintly smiling image of our own ego. We think of St. Ignatius of Loyola, founder of the Jesuits, who said humbly at the end of his life that if the Society of Jesus were disbanded, it would take him only fifteen minutes to become peaceful with that event, even though he had given most of his life to the building up and formation of that community. He refused to make an idol even out of his most significant work. Not all of us manage to be that detached, but we dimly recognize that we will never be fulfilled or centered by any thing.

Relationship to others

It is in our relationships with others that we more closely approximate human potential, our meaning and fulfillment. With others we experience one of the most beautiful and growth-producing gifts of God. The deep, intimate bond between two persons who love each other profoundly provides the closest analogy to and stepping-stone towards our relationship with the Lord. In a truly loving marriage, or in any intimate friendship, we may truly be ourselves. We feel loved, accepted, free to say anything we want without fear of rejection or neglect. We discover who we are and become who we are meant to be as others love us into our own identity. We would never know that it was all right to make mistakes, all right to fail, unless we had experienced those wonderful friends who have seen us flop and still have loved us.

Because we are loved, we will be understood, provided with the courage to share the deepest core of our being and, in the process, to discover that core ourselves. We receive the gift of self from others. We become, in religious language, sacraments to each other as we discover ourselves in relationship. In every relationship of love among human persons, the Spirit is mysteriously present. Good relationships are the context and the atmosphere in which God is to be found.

Still, even in this marvelous relationship, this gift from God, the other does not and cannot become absolute. Friend or spouse can die, or change, or let us down. Even the most excellent marital relationship cannot be made the total core of our life because another human cannot fulfill every need in us, cannot totally live up to our expectations and desires. To put so much pressure on any relationship would risk destroying it or us. Only the relationship with a transcendent other, with God, will ultimately provide our meaning.

Relationship with God

So we assert again that to pray is gradually to enter into a deeply personal relationship with God, one that provides an increasingly transforming and intimate centering and fulfilling of our lives.

For many people who do not really pray, God is not a person but only a kind of atmosphere, an ambience, a context for their lives. Our efforts to say prayers or go to church remain not unlike the initial entering into a house of someone we have heard a great deal about but never personally met. We observe the decor, the choice of colors, the presence of fresh flowers on a table, the types of books on the shelves, perhaps the smell of fresh bread baking. All these give an impression of, a feeling for, the person who lives in the house. How different when the owner enters and we meet the warm and gracious reality. It is thus that prayer really becomes a response on our part, a vital relationship with one who cherishes and cares for us as if we were the only one who existed. This communion gives life to us in a way different from every other, less satisfying relationship.

Sometimes this meeting happens in a moment of crisis. Sometimes it happens in the ordinary flow of our lives. But if we pray, open ourselves to the possibility, are quiet and able to wait, it does happen. We do meet, and nothing is ever the same again.

Whoever eats me will draw life from me
(John 6:57b)

No loving human being, no matter how fond of the other, could ask the spouse or friend to draw life and existence—the person's very being—from him or her. Only immature and adolescent human loves would ever make such promises or demands. Yet this is precisely what Christ asks and promises. In the biblical passage that begins this chapter, Jesus reveals to his disciples and to us his intention of giving his whole being as the core and meaning of our existence. Consider that chapter carefully. The subject matter is not simply the Eucharist, as we have usually contextualized it, but rather our entire relationship with Jesus, as all prayer and all entrance into friendship with him envisages it.

Our society faces two unanswered, perhaps unanswerable, questions: When does life begin? When does life end? For the Jews, with a simple physiology, the answer was obvious. Life was signed by flesh and blood. If you lived, there was blood in your veins; when you died, only a skeleton remained. The presence of flesh on bones and blood in veins was equivalent to life. What Jesus says to us in this passage becomes clear: "Take my life into you. Let me live in you." His disciples do not understand his words, and many walk away. Those who stay do so not because the possibility of what he asks seems clear but because they believed in *him.* So can we. His followers always and everywhere literally draw life from Christ and, to this end, eat him. He asks us to become the body by eating the body, taking on his life. His blood flows through our veins, his flesh takes shape on our bones. No other relationship could ever be so close. No other friendship could ever ask such response. In prayer we constantly reaffirm this process of lifelong assimilation.

Each time we celebrate the Eucharist we hear the words: "Do this in remembrance of me." All prayer calls us to remember the Lord's uncondi-tioned love and to act out that remembrance. Christ calls us to be drawn into his own action and life so deeply that we too become Eucharist. He in-vites us to parallel his own life, to do with our lives what he did with his—to teach, to heal, to challenge, but mostly to love all others. Personal prayer, a response within this unique relationship, invites us to become more aware of and open to what God wants to do in us for the sake of others. Mother Teresa of Calcutta puts it succinctly: "Let the people eat you up." Be as vulnerable to others as God is to you in Jesus, for he lives in you. The reassuring smile and the forgiving embrace become more than symbols: they are sacraments, for they express and convey the person and per-sonality of Jesus behind the action we perform.

Each of us will do this uniquely because we are unique persons. Paradoxically, the more closely we are drawn into Christ's life, the more our own personality emerges. Losing ourselves in him, we find ourselves. Insofar as we know God (in the biblical sense, in intimacy, intercourse, the act of love), we begin to know our true selves. To those who draw life from Christ, the individual true self is gradually revealed, and the totality of existence finds meaning.

Two people may, for example, spend a year praying over and being touched and called by the Gospel readings for the day. The same passages are prayed and pondered. The same Jesus is invited into the whole of the pray-er's life. One may be constantly struck by the special love of Jesus for the most needy, most outcast, most fragile of our world—the prostitute, the leper, the tax collector. Something strikes a cord responsive in her personal call and self-understanding. That is the Jesus she can become, and she does. Another is struck by the constant nature-images that Jesus speaks of (fig trees and lilies of the field, a field white for the harvest, a net full of fish), his sensitivity both to nature and to people. He recognizes something of himself and realizes that Jesus invites him into this same awareness, this same sensitivity. Two people, praying with the same passages, experience two quite different transformations. And the possibilities are endless, as numerous as the persons who dare to enter into this relationship.

This personhood which Christ unfolds to me in personal prayer is the gift I make to Christ and to his body, the community, because by this I bring something no one else can contribute. I can serve others the way no one else can. This gift of identity in Christ speaks more of a quality of life than of a specific ministry or life-form. It is present in priest or poet, wife or wayfarer, homebody or extrovert. Whatever I do can speak to others of Christ because of who I am—in Christ.

Reverse identification

Through solitary prayer and the response that prayer is within this transforming relationship, we are not only invited to become Christ's presence, his body and blood, but we are also enabled to see others reflecting the same reality back to us. We see Jesus in the flesh and blood of all with whom we come in contact. It is not so much that Jesus is *disguised* as poor, unemployed, or politically oppressed—hungry, naked, or in prison—as that such persons dramatically reveal his presence to us. We begin to see him everywhere and respond to him everywhere. "Insofar as you did this to one of the least of these brothers [or sisters] of mine, you did it to me" (Matt 25:40). "Saul, Saul, why are you persecuting me?" (Acts 22:7)

Assimilation into Christ

Since all prayer flows into and out of the Eucharist, we may consider the language of the Eucharist as descriptive of the actuality of all prayer. Within the

Eucharistic Prayer we recall the words of Jesus at table with his friends—he *took* the bread, *blessed* it, *broke* it, *gave* it to those at table with him. Taking, blessing, breaking, and giving constitute the dynamics of our prayerful assimilation into Christ. We take and are taken, bless and are blessed, break and are broken, give and are given.

Each day we offer ourselves to the Lord in solitary prayer, presenting our lives—our concerns, fears, emptiness, vulnerability—and asking God to transform us more fully into his presence. We take ourselves. He takes us. We are held in his hands. We become not our own but his.

IIe consecrates and blesses us in baptism, religious vows, marriage, and the everyday sanctity of our lives. And we bless and praise God for his lavish gifting of us, his children. We bless and thank him for friends, for failure, for faith and challenge. Like Jesus, we are grateful for God's revealing in our lives what may be hidden from the learned, clever, or sophisticated. All prayer is *Eucharist* ("thanksgiving"), for in all prayer there is explicit or implicit gratitude for God's faithfulness.

We break and are broken. Out of prayer we make even painful choices because they are the loving thing to do. We move to a new city or a new job because we feel called, even though we leave pieces of our heart behind. We say goodbye to friends who leave our religious community or who give up on a marriage that is not working. And we go on, in pain, because we know that this is what we are called to do. We experience loss of reputation, respect, or apparent freedom because we speak the words of God in a world that chooses to stay deaf. One way or another, gradually or with fierce immediacy, we are broken. Our false self is broken in the aridity of the prayer of faith as we stare into darkness with nothing for our ego to lay claim to. The fruit of our prayer is to allow us to be broken further as we stand against sexism, racism, nuclear arms, or religious oppression. We respond prayerfully, refusing to conform to cultural standards, declining to compromise basic Christ-values. We learn obedience by the things that we suffer. We are broken.

Only then can we give and be given. This is the climax of all Christian prayer, for there is no authentic prayer that does not spill over into lives of service and the sharing of love in compassion, laughter, tears, understanding, healing. Like Christ himself, we give. By him we are given. We freely lay down our lives, that is, his life (John 10:17–18).

Prayer enables us to change ourselves into another or to be changed by that other as we radically give ourselves into Christ's hands. Prayer then becomes a continuum, an ongoing action that Jesus and I are doing and becoming. Prayer becomes not only this presence, this person within me, but my presence, my person within him. Wherever I am, there he is. Where he goes, I go with him. The Eucharist is the prayerful sign that in *communion* with others, our lives reflect not just our own lives but the life of the risen Christ himself. Life itself marvelously unfolds the incarnation in us daily as we progressively take on Christ's own life in prayer.

Personal prayer changes me into the Jesus I receive in that prayer until I become his presence in the world. To encounter God in all that is deepest in myself each day is to ask that God gradually turn me into the image of the Son who prays in me. This he does by gradually healing the dark side of my being and inviting me to participate more and more in his life, ultimately transforming me into who I most truly am. My prayer expresses much more than I can be conscious of. It is an attachment to Christ and a consent to be the person I am called to be in *Christ*. This is the self I am so ambivalent about. This is the self I am so afraid of becoming because it is my real self, created by an act of faith before God, in relationship, in response to that God. It is the self I need so much to be. I become God's work of art (Eph 2:10).

4

Eucharist
as Prayerful Response

*They who eat the break and drink the cup un-
worthily, not thinking about the body of Christ
and what it means, eat and drink God's judgment upon themselves, for they trifle with the
death of Christ.*

1 Cor 11:27

We have just reflected on the deep reality of prayer
as a response within a relationship. All prayer is
response. Since God has first loved us, we love one
another. We accept, we experience, God's love
over and over, and out of that received gift, we respond. The Eucharist, like every sacramental,
liturgical action of the Church, is first, last, and
always prayer. The Eucharist is a communal response to God's love for us as a people.

We could speak of many aspects of this central
prayer of ourselves as a people, but we will focus
on only one—the Eucharist as *response* to the freely
given love of God. This is no tangent to the

mystery, for, as pointed out earlier, the very name *Eucharist* means "thanksgiving": our formal, celebrational, liturgical, communal way of accepting and appreciating the love given us in Jesus Christ.

We start where we usually end. What constitutes the most important words of the Eucharist? Most tend to focus on the words: "This is my body, . . . my blood." Or they may say, "The body of Christ," to which we say, "Amen." The more sophisticated may suggest that our "Amen" to the final part of the Eucharistic Prayer, "Through him, with him, in him, . . ." summarizes the entirety and is, therefore, most significant. More sophisticated still, the biblically astute worshiper who understands the dynamic of Word-Eucharist may suggest that the most important words are the proclamation of the Gospel, the word by which we are formed into a people who can dare to say "Our Father."

For the purpose of this discussion and out of deep conviction, we suggest that the most significant words of the eucharistic celebration are: "The Mass is ended. Go in peace to love and serve the Lord." The very word *Mass,* which for centuries has been our Catholic name for the Eucharist, means, literally, that from which "we are sent." What we do after we leave, how we live out the mystery in the marketplace, the extent to which we not only have received but have become the body and blood of Christ—these are the measures of how authentic our prayer in church truly was.

The ways in which we weave Eucharist into the fabric of our lives indicate how fruitful our liturgical prayer was. The Eucharist cannot remain only something we attend. It is something we do and, more important, something we become. The response that overtakes our lives validates the experience of prayer. The significant question regarding any prayer is not "How did I feel when I prayed?" but rather, "How did I love when I lived?"

We can say the same thing another way. The early Fathers of the Church, less squeamish than we are, sometimes had the audacity and the wisdom to suggest that the best way to understand Communion (Eucharist) was in comparison with the act of sexual love between a truly loving and committed husband and wife. The best way, conversely, to understand human sexuality was by comparison with the Eucharist.

In sexual love within such a relationship, two people blend into one, celebrating in sign and symbol all that preceded this moment. They bring to the marriage bed everything that has constituted their lives and their love up to this moment. They also pledge themselves to one another into a future yet unknown. They reaffirm their covenant. They say with lips and bodies that they will be present to one another tomorrow and through an endless succession of tomorrows. They celebrate both past and future in a joyous now. They are literally and figuratively naked to each other, open to each other, giving and receiving, vulnerable and accepting the vulnerability of each other. They have spoken to one another, grown in knowledge of one another through dialogue and sharing of their word. They have undoubtedly seen to whatever reconciliation may have been necessary between them. They have eaten and drunk at the same table. All these prepared them for the union of this moment.

The comparison with the Eucharist is obvious. The point to be made is that no couple evaluates the worth of their marriage nor the full effect of their lives by looking only at their sexual experience, however significant that experience may be. They evaluate their marriage by the fullness of life, joy, and peace, and by their ability to enter dynamically into their world. Similarly, in the Eucharist, what we do with it matters. We evaluate how fruitful the celebration has been by how we return to our world, fully empowered by our union with Jesus. Have we been more dynamically transformed by gratitude, more graciously peacefilled by the power of the Spirit?

In the remainder of this chapter, we will look at the various parts that make up the Eucharist— our prayerful, liturgical celebration—in terms of communal worship and that which promotes communal involvement and communal response. We want to look at Eucharist as prayer, for all prayer is response. We answer the question: How do we celebrate Eucharist in a way that involves the community and fosters a response from it? We are not mere witnesses, but a priestly people, offering together the one salvific act of Christ. We insist again that the Eucharist cannot be celebrated the same way in each community, nor in the same community the same way every day. Our lives, dreams, hopes, fears, and reasons for coming together—that is, our mood and mystery— constantly change, and so must our way of saying thanks to the Lord's presence in our lives.

Gathering for worship

Many contemporary liturgists suggest that we need to pay primary attention to what goes on before the Eucharist starts. What happens at home and at the church before people come together for Sunday Mass? We will not dwell on this at great length, but any community would do well to emphasize that those who come are coming to do something and do it together. Has anyone read the Scripture for that celebration before arriving? Does anyone come with questions about the readings or their meanings in our lives? Do people arrive early enough to be really present, to greet friends and neighbors, to enter into the mood for this act of prayerful presence to God and one another? How often people arrive ten to fifteen minutes before a concert or a play. They get settled, read the program, admire the set, listen to the mood music, prepare for the drama. What a difference it would make if we arrived at Mass in this way! Do we greet each other at the door as we walk in, introduce ourselves to strangers or newcomers? Do we prepare for music, practice at least one piece to sing together? How amazing the celebration becomes when we practice responses, achieving some enthusiasm before the prayer begins. At a football game the cheerleaders practice one or two new cheers before the teams even take the field. The Eucharist is neither play nor game, but we learn from such activities how people come together and blend into community. From other groupings we learn to question how seriously we take what we profess to be the centrally most significant action of our day, or week, or life.

Music

We are not musicians and will not pretend to an expertise we do not have, but a word on music is necessary as part of our response in prayer at the Eucharist. It has become a verbal (if not functional) truism that one who sings prays twice. Cantor and choir have their proper roles, but we insist simply that for the Eucharist to be the prayer of a community, our gathering needs to have well-known responses that it sings together. Our sung response is often the only external way that a community enters fully into the entrance procession, the hearing of the word, the proclamation of the Eucharistic Prayer. Musicians understandably get tired of singing the same things a hundred times over, but the community hears them only on Sunday and needs to practice to make them truly its own. Familiarity is far more important than variety in community responses.

Reconciliation rite

Two somewhat opposite understandings of this first stance at the Eucharist prevail. The "Lord Have Mercy" was probably intended to be a hymn of praise to the mercy of God, sung as the celebrant and community gathered. It has become in many communities a moment of recognition of our stance before God as sinners needing that mercy, that healing, right now. Whatever the historical situation, there is now a psychological aptness to a moment of quiet prayer, a prayer for forgiveness and healing at the outset of the Eucharist. Just as any two friends often take a moment to repair any small or large wounds of the past before beginning lunch—or a meeting or any other activity together —so any community benefits from the articulated realization that we come together as less than perfect people. Almost every meeting of friends begins with words like "I'm sorry I didn't call you," or "I meant to write you a note," or "It's a shame it's been so long." We need to get the "junk" out of the way to enable us to become present to one another. Moreover, it is good that we come together clearly as imperfect people,

65

acknowledging that we are a pilgrim Church, a community needing God's love, for we have not yet responded as we would like. It is important that we all know that others as well as ourselves come here not because we deserve it but because we need it. Henri Nouwen has often pointed out that the beginning of intimacy is the sharing of our weakness. Because we all stand in need of the love of the Lord, we stand in need of each other.

In a more profound way, the reconciliation rite at the beginning of our prayer, though a very minor moment in the whole, takes seriously the words of Jesus in Matthew's Gospel: "If you bring your gifts to the altar and there remember that you have something against your brother or sister, go first and make peace with them, and then come and offer your gifts" (Matt 5:23–24). The entire Eucharist is a healing, reconciling prayer of people coming together before their God, but a momentary pause at the outset recognizes that the basic Christian stance is always to realize that though we are imperfect, though we are sinners, we will go on to celebrate the far more important reality that we are sinners who are called, loved, chosen, and redeemed. Care can be taken that this initial rite be carried out sincerely and honestly. What are the failings of this people at this time of its history? What will the readings call us to look at critically today? Where do we individually and as a people see ourselves deeply in need of the Lord's mercy?

Gloria

The early part of the rite of the Eucharist seems cluttered at present. If an entrance song of praise has been sung, it becomes repetitious to sing another so soon. Still, one of the wonderful things about the proclamation "Glory to God in the highest" is the immediate connection with the hope for "peace to his people on earth." We respond in praise to God that these two realities are inseparable. This is not a bad point to make in the beginning or wherever it can be made.

Liturgy of the Word

A major task to become again "A People of the Book" faces the Catholic community. We need to pay careful attention to the proclamation of the word in ways that invite attention and response. We need to learn to reverence the word of God. We might begin to promote this by burning all missalettes! The word is spoken and heard, not read privately by each individual in the congregation. Readers need to be well prepared. The text should be nearly memorized and proclaimed to the congregation with the enthusiasm, understanding, and intelligence with which a storyteller weaves a spell on an audience by recalling the greatest of stories ever told.

One pictures the typical Sunday congregation. Some hold their loose-leaf missalettes in their hands. Some are reading the bulletin. As the readings are offered, people continue to drift into church, genuflect, kneel for a moment of prayer— all this even though God is trying to speak to them through the lector. The noise, movement, and lack of attention during the Scripture readings would never occur during the silent sacredness we traditionally give to the eucharistic narrative, especially the remembered words of consecration. Yet God is equally present in each. Years of hearing that we were "on time" for Mass if we arrived before the veil came off the chalice have conditioned us to make this terribly important Scripture time insignificant. Perhaps we need to remember that in most congregations now the veil is off the chalice before the celebration even begins. More seriously, we need to create an invitation to attentive, responsive listening. We bring the book in with reverence and place it prominently before the congregation as the central focus for the first half of our prayer. At the proper time the reader is invited to stand in place until the whole room is still as all eyes focus on the one who will speak of God to them. Constant eye contact during the reading, as well as familiarity with the text, followed by a lengthy silence after the reading, all create an atmosphere of importance, solemnity, significance.

Liturgy is prayer, and we need to emphasize the moments of prayer. Each reading deserves contemplative attention, silence, and listening with the heart. Each hearer will perhaps ponder a different word or phrase. Our response within the Liturgy of the Word may well be simply thirty seconds of respectful, meditative silence after the first reading, after the second reading, and after the homily, while we struggle to internalize the word we have heard.

We have done an informal study and discovered what we already knew, namely, that if the responsorial psalm is read, the entire congregation spends the time trying to remember what the refrain for the psalm is. We have a whimsical fantasy that the refrain will someday be: ''How happy upon the mountains are the feet of the one who brings good news to the people, proclaiming justice, righteousness, and good will to God and all his people, as long as life shall last among us.'' The entire congregation will throw up their hands in collective despair—a despair felt for a long, long time. Simply put, the psalm is meant to be sung as a meditative refrain, a way of being—with the themes of the readings for the day. If the psalm is not sung, let us be silent rather than clutter up minds and hearts with more unnecessary words.

In all of the above, we cannot help but return to the earlier reflection on the relationship between the whole action of the Eucharist and the human act of love. Every married couple would assert with deep conviction that the sexual act, in order to be integrated, whole, fulfilling, and satisfying, needs to be part of an entire relationship in which dialogue, conversation, growing knowledge, and

69

love of one another constantly reaffirms what their sexual act signifies. Communion of bodies without the sharing of a word is empty and ultimately deadly. Any relationship in which we said the same words and performed identically the same actions every time we met would soon flounder and die. We have all had friends who called us on the phone day after day with the same laments, same stories, same jokes. We soon lose interest, do crossword puzzles, or make out grocery lists as we listen to the same old thing again. The Liturgy of the Word offers the diversity, freshness, and newness that keeps our communion alive. It is never an ancient word but always a new word to a new people, today. If our communion with the Lord and one another is to be fruitful, it must necessarily be preceded by a careful hearing of the God who loves and calls us. The Liturgy of the Eucharist *is* response to the Liturgy of the Word.

Central to the word-dimension of our prayerful celebration is the homily. Entire books can and should be written on the importance of the exposition of Scripture to the community. Though much work needs to be done, the opportunity to change the quality of homiletics evades most Catholics. Still, in terms of our concern with prayerful response, some things can be said. First, we suggest that all who share in the Eucharist would do well to prepare their own homily. If all the worshipers at a given Eucharist had already considered what to say about the texts to themselves, or to the community, our energy would rise, our attentiveness would thrive, and the homily would achieve its purpose, whatever the quality of the words actually spoken by the homilist.

Second, it seems important to reflect on what we really can expect from these eight-to-ten important minutes. There is no time for adequate teaching; we will not learn the contents of our beliefs from a succession of homilies. We need adult education classes, Bible studies, and reading for this. Neither will every homily speak to every person in the same way and with the same force. No one can totally relate to an audience ranging in age from eight to eighty, with grade school education to graduate degrees, touching every point on the liberal-conservative spectrum. What can be done, though apparently more modest, is significant.

One can speak of God's activity in one's own life, let the word of God address that life, tell of personal fears and uncertainties, and indicate how God's word hopes us out of cynicism or despair. One can help others experience the word of God as saving, sometimes comforting, sometimes challenging, but always relevant at least to one very real life, prompting response from at least one very real heart. The homilist can lead a community from word to Eucharist, indicating how the word proclaimed today prepares us to need more deeply, or depend upon, or celebrate, the reality of Jesus Christ whom we are about to offer and receive.

One can lead others from the word of God to the God of the word, now enfleshed and present among us. The homilist can lead us to eucharistic response. Homilists should receive our encouragement to do so, our congratulations when they succeed, and our gentle correction when they fail.

Creed

Again, although a profession of faith after the Liturgy of the Word and before the Eucharist fits psychologically, the ritualistic recitation of a creedal formula rarely fulfills its possibilities. How can a community make this faith response an honest, personal response? We generally manage to sound quite like a freight train going ever more rapidly downhill. We need to do it well and honestly, or not at all.

We speak of a renewal of our baptismal profession: "This is the faith of the Church. We are proud to profess it, in Christ Jesus our Lord." Perhaps we can imitate the baptismal style and profess our faith in dialogic form:

Leader: Do you believe in God?

Congregation: We do believe!

L: Do you believe in Jesus Christ, God's Son, our brother, who lived among us, died as one of us, and lives still?

C: We do believe!

L: Do you believe that the Spirit of Jesus still lives in us, bonds us together, creates a Church, an everlasting communion of God's people, and continually calls us to the forgiveness of sins?

C: Yes, we do believe!

Perhaps one member of the community could say loudly each poignant phrase of the creed as others responded Yes!

However we may respond in faith, we would do well as a community to let the words be a truly prayerful response in the light of the word recently reflected on.

Prayer of the Faithful

We are funny people. We just finish recalling God's mighty deeds on our behalf. We prepare to give solemn thanks for them. In between we take a moment to ask for more. We pause and voice what we do not have yet, what we want, what we still hope for.

What do we do when we pray for God's continued blessings for ourselves and for others? Does not God already love us totally? Is God unaware of our needs? Do we think that by raising our common voices we will change God, get God to love us more, love us better, be even more gracious to us?

We suggest that there is an intimacy in asking and, further, that we ask not so much to change God as to change ourselves. There is a deep intimacy implied in asking help from God or anyone. We do not ask easily. Only in deep trust and close friendship do I dare say "Can I borrow your car?"

73

or "Can you help me with a problem?" Most of us are able to plead or beg or make known our own drastic vulnerability only in the wake of a deep awareness of already being loved. We long for independence. We speak dependence grudgingly. The prayers of the faithful people are an intimate response growing out of our nurtured faith. These prayers speak a corporate dependence far more significant than any expectation that God will accomplish what we pray for without our having to be involved.

We do not so much expect God to change as to invite God to change us, empower us, and enable us to bring to be what we pray for. Because we live in him, we remind ourselves of the "not yet" in our lives in the light of the "already now" we have recently reaffirmed. The prayers of the faithful are indeed prayer, important prayer, focusing on the expressed, felt, longed-for needs of a people, needs that we hope to do our part to fulfill.

Perhaps in this moment of prayer, more than any other, we call to our communal mind the business left unfinished that we must be about when we leave. So we "do" the prayer with care and attention. The community is involved in formulating the prayers, which grow out of the Scripture and the homily just completed. They relate us to the eucharistic moment towards which we move. They come also from recent life within the larger and smaller community, our own successes and sicknesses, and the secular and religious needs of our neighborhood, city, and world. We take care not to focus only on ourselves. The hungry and the homeless, the embattled and oppressed, the refugee and jobless, are part of our concern. Finally, we couch the formulation of these prayers in words showing that we do not expect God to settle things alone, but with our cooperation.

Presentation of gifts

People from the parish bring forward the bread and wine. Ushers move through the congregation, collecting money. A song rises amidst the rustling of paper and clattering of coins. Distraction abounds during what appears to be a rest period between the central moments of our prayer. It is a recess while the table is set, the banquet is prepared, and things used for Mass are placed on the altar. But the bread and wine are not things, and we are not waiting and watching. We offer not only our money but ourselves.

Deeply fixed in the Catholic imagination is the belief that bread and wine will become the body and blood—what once was bread becomes the flesh of Jesus, what once was wine, his blood. Though true, this offers the right answer to the wrong, or less significant, question. Few Catholics (our imagination colored by Reformation disputes and questions asking *what* is there) realize that the pertinent question ought to ask *who* is present on the altar. The bread and wine are never truly present as bread and wine, but as "firstfruits," the first part of the life of a people. The bread and wine are ours; they are our selves. Bread and wine are brought to the altar because we are brought to the altar. We place ourselves—our needs, hopes, dreams, lives, deaths, joys, and sorrows—here to be transformed by the loving presence of Jesus. They will be given back to us, empowering us more than we ever have been before. *Who* is present on the altar? We are. *Who* is present there? Jesus Christ. He takes over not just bread and wine but us. He assumes our mortal lives and we receive him to carry out the meaning. We become who he is, as he became who we are. Jesus pitches his tent among us, lives, dies, and rises to new life. We share in his new life and become, like the bread and wine, what we have never been before, the very life, the body of Christ.

Because of this reality we hear Paul saying the words that began this chapter. We need to think about the body of Christ and what it means when we eat and drink the body and blood. We need to know that the body of Christ is not the consecrated bread alone but the people who will receive—who have already received—this bread. We are the body of Christ, members of one another. Unless we recognize the body of Christ in one another, in people now presenting themselves to be renewed in and reminded of this reality, we will not later recognize the body of Jesus under forms of bread and wine on the altar.

In some respects, the presentation of gifts remains a minor action in our prayer. We should not dwell on it. Still, somehow we want to symbolize the terribly important reality that the gifts are ours, our selves.

The custom of bringing money forward at this time, though seemingly gross, appropriately symbolizes our society, but it can be used as more than a convenient way to collect needed church revenue. The collection represents our own "first-fruits," a giving of ourselves when we present our dollar or our dime. A shock from time to time might help. Many have heard of the parish in which the celebrant one day removed 10 percent of the collection and burned it before the congregation—wasted it, destroyed it, gave it to God. Perhaps less dramatic and more pragmatic, we could allocate some percentage of the money to some need of the larger church or world, capturing our response of giving of our selves, our lives, at least our funds, in the name of Jesus to his people and not merely to ourselves.

However we convey the response we hope to make, we know we are a people who have heard the word of God, have believed in it again, now bringing ourselves to be a part of his paschal, Easter mysteries, to cooperate with his saving act. We offer ourselves with him, through life and death and resurrection (his own and ours), to building the kingdom of the Father.

Eucharistic Prayer

The Eucharistic Prayer primarily proclaims our act of remembrance of God's faithful deeds in the past. We tell again the story of God's love, especially in Jesus, and most particularly when Jesus took bread and wine and covenanted himself with us forever. Somehow we need to make this a prayerful response of the people, though it appears to be something the celebrant says as others listen. Much less should it be something the celebrant reads out of a big book while the people read the same thing out of a little book. This prayer of remembrance forms us as an Easter people. We involve ourselves in it as a community. We sing full-throated responses ("Holy, holy, holy Lord . . . ," "Christ has died," "Amen."). We also need, perhaps, to stand attentively rather than kneel humbly. We are part of the proclamation; this is our prayer, spoken by our voice. The priest is one of us, not other than we. He speaks far more as the voice of the community than as the voice of Jesus, even as he repeats the words of Jesus. More precisely, he is the voice of the body of Christ, which is Jesus and also we.

Notice also, aside from the remembrance-dimension of the Eucharistic Prayer, the continual plea for harmony among all who share this bread and wine. The response to God that this prayer evokes we discover in our response to one another. We remember the body of Christ (literally, we put back together the torn members of this body), prepare to receive the body of Christ, and long for deeper unity with the body of Christ.

Communion rite

The culmination of our prayer, communion with our God and one another, breaks into three distinct parts, each with a significant dimension of responsive involvement on our part. We begin with a communal recitation of the Lord's Prayer. Recall the former introduction to this prayer: "Formed by the word of God, we dare to say." Because we are a people caught up into the word of God, we can boldly call God "Father" and know that he is *our* Father, not merely *mine*. This prayer responds to everything Jesus has revealed to us about the creating, nurturing, life-giving, life-sustaining, Father-Mother God. The prayer becomes, then, not just a plea to God but a commitment on our part. We do not expect God instantly, or even eventually, to drop a kingdom on us from above. Rather, in union with Jesus and living in his Spirit, we commit ourselves to the building of that kingdom, the doing of his will, the sharing of the daily bread needed for people to live, the forgiving of sins that enables the Lord's forgiveness to touch us. The whole of the Eucharist coalesces in this prayer, a prayer that most deeply responds to God and to God's people.

The next moment of the Communion rite as presently constituted is the sign of peace. This greeting could be done (and often is) elsewhere in our prayer. Some prefer it after the reconciliation rite as a sign of the peace of forgiveness. Some prefer it at the presentation of gifts, fleshing out in gesture the theme of making peace with one another before we bring our gifts to the altar. We would uphold the deeply theological and psychological fittingness of offering that gesture now, just before Communion.

We turn and open ourselves to one another, receiving the body of Christ as it comes to us in our brothers and sisters before we receive that body from the altar. The sign of peace helps us to make specific the connection between the body of Christ on the altar and in the community. In the passage which began this chapter, Paul was deeply concerned with the way the Corinthians came together for the Lord's Supper. Some brought their own dinner; some brought wine to drink. Poorer people brought nothing. Some ate too much while others went hungry, and some got drunk. It was not the Lord's Supper they were celebrating. They did not recognize "the body," that is, they did not reverence each other as they gathered to proclaim the death of Jesus till he came. Paul warns them that they trifle with the death of Christ and eat and drink unworthily, not recognizing the body and what it means. Recall that Paul's Christian life began with this recognition. When he persecuted

Christians, he persecuted Christ. The Lord hurled him to the ground and asked, "Why are you persecuting me?" We imagine Paul responding in confusion, "Who are you? I'm just out killing a few Christians!" His relationship with Jesus began with the realization that Jesus lived in his followers. To love them was to love him; to hurt them was to hurt him. Paul never forgot. He constantly reaffirmed that Christ lives in us.

How fitting, then, immediately before Communion, to turn to one another in a gesture of peace, an embrace, a sign, a sacrament that indicates that we wish for others the peace we want for ourselves, the peace of Christ, the peace the world cannot give, the peace we do not give as part of the world but as part of Christ. This peace surpasses understanding, breaks barriers, commits us to begin again and anew to love one another as Christ loves us.

We then turn back to the altar, the bread, and the cup, responding to God's invitation to let him live more deeply in us. We have stressed for so long the receptivity of this act of Communion that we would do well to put equal stress on the response implied in this reception. We open our hands, our mouths, and our hearts to receive the flesh and blood of Jesus. We open ourselves, as we do in any prayer, to letting him truly live in us. We lose ourselves in him in order to find ourselves, as we indicated in the previous chapter. We accept the invitation and the call, the challenge and the gift, to be the hands and heart of Christ in the world. Nowhere is it more clear than in this act of Communion that the Eucharist is prayer and that prayer is responding to the transforming love of God for me in Jesus. We commit ourselves to becoming what we receive.

Dismissal

We come to the final and what we have called the most significant moment of our prayer as a people, our Eucharist. We are sent (massed, missioned) back into the world from which we came. We are sent to be what we have proclaimed ourselves to be, a thankful people, the body of Christ. We "go to love and serve the Lord." We have prayed and have tried to respond to God in a variety of ways. We do not by any means deny the real presence but assert its many-sidedness. Jesus has been present to us and in us in far more ways than one.

We have met the Lord in the gathered community, for where two or three are gathered in his name, he is already in our midst (Matt 18:20). We have met the Lord in the pilgrim people of the penance rite. Jesus came to forgive sins, to assure us of the Father's forgiveness. His Spirit has breathed over us and, because we have forgiven one another, his forgiveness has been present to us, in us. We have met the Lord in the word proclaimed to us, the two-edged sword, the living word of God that will not return to God empty. We

82

have met the Lord as a community of thanks, a eucharistic people, gathered in his name to be fed by his real life. We have met the Lord in the presence of a priest who stands, in part, in Jesus' name as his sacramental presence in our midst, repeating again his words of promise and of love.

Having met the Lord, truly present to us in this variety of ways, having readjusted our vision and seen more clearly what we otherwise would have missed—his almost ubiquitous presence among us in this church—we go now to meet him everywhere. He will be continually present to us in our world—in the hungry who cry out to be fed, the thirsty longing for a drink, prisoners in jail, the naked, and the homeless. He is in them all. Having met Christ here in prayer, we go to meet Christ and to respond to his presence in absolutely everything, everyone.

Though the Eucharist is only one form of prayer in the Church, it is our central prayer—that into which all of Christian life flows, and out of which all Christian life comes. It is not a passive prayer, not a ritual act that magically saves. It is prayer involving a response. It is our response within a love relationship remembered, celebrated, deepened—one from which we go renewed, revivified, refleshed.

5

Prayer as Radical

I set before you life or death, blessing or curse.
Choose life, then, so that you and your de-
scendants may live, in the love of Yahweh
your God, obeying his voice, clinging to him.
Deut 30:19–20a

In chapters 1 and 2 we spoke of life and all that life connotes. A problem occurs because death and the path to death simulate life. The existence of sin will always mean that what looks like death may well be life and what appears to be life-giving is often death-dealing. The very attraction of sin is that is purports to offer life. The classic description of evil (sin) as the absence of good makes us wonder why anyone would then choose sin. But we are seduced precisely because all sin has some aspect of good which attracts us. Not all good is absent.

In order to avoid a difficult situation or suffering because of my failure, I tell a lie. The lie is convenient and convenience seems good, especially at the time. Only when the lie is discovered and an

85

important relationship has been damaged or destroyed do I realize that some good was absent, that I chose a lesser good when I could have been honest and strengthened the relationship.

I am sexually attracted to someone other than my wife. She is lovely, charming, and cares about me. I enter into an extramarital affair—not because it is bad, but precisely because it looks like good. Only later do I realize the absence of good in the totality of my life as children, wife, and other-woman all are injured by my infidelity.

We spend enormous sums of money to build bigger, better, more powerful weapons to protect us. It is obviously a good thing to be protected. We may only realize the sin, the absence of good, when the bombs begin to go off and our civilization is destroyed.

We always choose evil under the guise of good, however dim the good, however out of step with the other goods of our lives. For many of us, it seems that sin really is good and is only *called* evil because some arbitrary God decides so. We imagine adultery would be all right except that we are commanded not to commit it; lying would be fine, but God says No. The reality is that sin, like virtue, has its own reward. Sin, if it is truly sin, really does lack the fullness of good that makes it evil. Things are not wrong because God says so, but God says so because they are wrong—they really are destructive of our humanity, injurious to others, or disruptive of the human community.

Still, over and over again, we frail humans recognize ourselves settling for lesser goods, less happiness, less human fulfillment. We come to resonate with Paul's lament: "I cannot understand my own behavior. I fail to carry out the things I want to do, and I find myself doing the very things I hate" (Rom 7:15).

Sin is also unique to each person. My particular personality is not yours, and my inclination to evil is not yours, either. We each wrestle with our particular demons, our personal propensity to laziness or dishonesty, injustice or timidity, insensitivity or abrasiveness.

In prayer, we put on Christ in order to become ever more sensitive to the authentic good in our own personal life and death issues. We pray in order to be changed, guided by God's love. Without prayer, we easily look around and see someone apparently weaker, more slothful, less loving than ourselves. But when we allow ourselves to be challenged by God, the facade crumbles. Sooner or later our sin confronts us, not just in the isolated single act of the moral theology manuals, but the deep, pervasive sinfulness within us. It is at this point that prayer has become radical; it literally gets at the root of our life, uproots and reroots us in Christ, helps us choose life. We have said that prayer is a response to God in our very real life. It also touches that life and that response in radical fashion. Note, however, that letting God's love, God's word, confront us and change us is not to be overcome with guilt, mired in self-recrimination, overwhelmed with self-hatred. Rather it is to recognize love—love to which we *can* respond. Rather than paralyzing, this prayer experience is freeing, inviting.

Still it can be a terrifying experience for some, especially those who have led a good and proper life, who have tried so hard to be right. It is frightening to realize that left to myself I am so imperfect, so ridden with inescapable sin. For others, the experience is less dramatic but no less real. For all who pray, eventually our life experience seems to connect with a kind of internal urging, demanding some kind of change. Life may go along peacefully for months or years until one day, in large or small areas of my life, the bottom drops out and I recognize myself as I am. I gradually become aware of the extremes to which I go to protect my image, or I experience a vague sense of anxiety, or I realize my loneliness and isolation, my inability to touch or be touched by others. My complacency is disturbed. Within these powerful stirrings, this profound awareness of the sin that is in me, lies the invitation to new life, to growth, to wholeness.

We name this experience *conversion, repentance,* or (in the Greek) *metanoia.* We cannot grow in our prayer relationship with God and others without this uprooting experience in which we will be immersed again and again. Regardless of what we may think of the quality of our prayer, whether we have constant consolation and occasional visions or perpetual dryness and a very distant God, this ongoing conversion is the infallible sign that our prayer is fruitful. If we pray, we will be changed. If we are not in any way changed, we are not praying —no matter how many hours we put in apparently doing so.

Regret, shame, sorrow

The call to conversion, to be other than we are, is initially very painful as we move from regret to shame to honest sorrow with which we begin to change.

We first experience an overwhelming feeling of *regret* and guilt, probably indicative of a chastened (deflated?) ego that failed to meet its own expectations. We experience not authentic sorrow but pride. "How could *I* have done that?" "How could *I* have been so blind for so long?" "I've always considered myself sensitive; how could *I* have been so destructive?" I am personally disappointed, dissatisfied, that I turned in such a poor performance, ruined my self-image, was unable to love as I would like.

When I begin to see the interpersonal ramifications of my acts, attitudes, or desires, my regret becomes more a sense of *shame.* I am embarrassed to have been the cause of someone else's pain. Often I find it difficult to forgive myself for what I have inflicted on others. I am nearly paralyzed at the realization of how my selfish acts affect friends, co-workers, members of my family, or have added to the injustice of the world. This transition from mere regret to shame becomes terribly important, for we cannot even begin to have a sense of sin until we discover what it means to love or be loved. We need to let other human persons become as important to us as ourselves. If we have not yet tasted, seen, or felt something of the love of others, we cannot sin, for sin is correlative to love. The commandment Jesus gives us is simple enough in theory: "Love one another as I have loved you" (John 15:12). Sin is the failure, the inability, to love. Until I am ashamed of how I have hurt another, how my actions have affected the lives of others, I do not truly begin to speak of sin.

But only gradually do we move from shame to real *sorrow,* conversion, and repentance. Though sorrow certainly involves developing our giftedness from God, and respecting and loving others, its meaning lies deeper. In sorrow, I am not the focus. I do not see primarily my regret, my shame. Real conversion centers on God. Repentance results from a deeper turning to God rather than a closer inspection of myself. I may know myself to be a sinner but, more important, I know God's call and love. The Lord is not as concerned with what I have done wrong as with how I may change in my capacity to grow in love. Like a sensitive artist, God chooses to use my imperfections to enhance his work of art. In my weakness I become God's to work in, work through. The radicality of prayer lies in my reliance on the power, love, mercy, and hope of God, despite and in the very face of my inadequacy. When I am weak, then I am strong (2 Cor 12:10). Authentic sorrow turns me from attention on myself (and consequent despair) to trust in God and the constant ability to change.

Frequent conversion

The process of conversion is neither a one-time-only nor a yearly Lenten project. Repentance happens many times. An endless series of larger and smaller conversions, inner revolutions and uprootings, leads to our transformation in Christ Jesus. We are never wholly transformed, never finished with our conversion. Faith is the readiness to enter more deeply into prayer, into the process of letting God shape us, stretch us, and lead us to new depths of trust, love, and freedom as we change our image of God, of ourselves, and of our entire reality.

The woman who was a sinner: vignette of prayer

The seventh chapter of St. Luke's Gospel (vv. 36–50) tells the powerful story of a sinful woman entering the house of Simon the Pharisee, falling to her knees before Jesus, washing his feet with her tears, and drying them with her hair. The tale tells us many things, but we would use it here as a vignette of prayer, bringing out two points.

Jesus tells the self-righteous Simon, indignant at the presence of this fallen woman in his house, that her many sins must have been forgiven her or she would not have shown such great love. The first point is that love follows forgiveness. Her ability to love so much, so desperately, so publicly, derives from her experience of having been loved. She already knew God's love, had experienced it in Jesus, or she could not have acted in this way. Had she not met and been deeply touched by the presence of this Jesus in her life, she would not have changed from the sinful woman Simon thought he knew to the sorrowful woman who fell at Jesus' feet.

Forgiveness is given, never earned. Despite who she had been, she had been loved. She did not make herself lovable, nor do we. We are loved first. The sinful woman's impassioned and moving desire to reverence the body of Jesus flows out of gratitude for and awe at the fact of being so profoundly and undeservedly loved. This sense is what healed her, allowed her to give herself to him, in what appeared bizarre to those who had never experienced such love.

Gradually, over time and out of prayer, the invitation to grow, to change, to become a new person in some area of our life, becomes a serene summons. The call produces, not feelings of anxiety or guilt, but a quiet desire to be more truly who God calls us to be. So an archbishop in El Salvador, praying over the reality of his life and the sufferings of his people, realizes he has not done enough to ease those sufferings. He throws himself into the arms of the Lord, in and through his people, and becomes a martyr for him and for them. It does not matter that we have nothing of ourselves because we have met a lover who gives us everything.

The second point in this simple, lovely story is that mission follows forgiveness. The consoling words Jesus utters to the woman, "Go in peace," become a kind of missioning to her and to us each time we experience the power of God's healing, forgiving love, whether that occurs alone in prayer or in the context of a sacramental celebration. This mission calls us to offer gratuitous forgiveness and acceptance to others, enables us to trust our own goodness, to forgive ourselves, and to believe in God's forgiveness. To freely forgive, and to honestly and prayerfully seek healing for others, is to reverence the body of Christ as did this once (but no longer) sinful woman.

Curing and Caring

In this account and in many other passages, Jesus concerned himself with caring, not with curing. We think of Jesus when we recall that sign in a high school counselor's office: "Don't *should* on me!" He cared for, loved, even teased to life the people he met. He was not out to reform them and force them to be different. They did not have to become something else in order to earn his care.

The cure results from the care, not vice-versa. Sadly enough, our reaction to those who fail to live up to our expectations for them, who hurt or ignore us, is to make them shape up or to get back at them. We may "bury the hatchet," but we tend to remember exactly where we buried it and find ourselves going back to it again. We accomplish nothing with a condescending attitude. Which one of us cannot recall the pain, the near impossibility, of trying to forgive ourselves when others refused to do so? No one helps us or cures us without first caring for us. Though it may evoke temporary conformity, criticism never promotes permanent change unless we already know that the critic loves us. A teacher, a parent, or a priest can only try to love, to care. Love cures; without it, we cannot.

This desire to care is life-giving. It does not rule out gentle confrontation but implies a genuine love for others. This love honestly seeks to listen, to affirm, to forgive, because we try to understand why and how and where the other honestly struggles. The ability to do this does not come easily, nor does it come from us. Only by being with the Lord over and over again in radically converting prayer do we take on that life which empowers us.

The recent play and film *The Elephant Man* encapsulates a deep human experience, a religious experience. It tells the true story of John Merrick, whose grotesque, distorted body veiled the spirit of a gentle, sensitive man. John was the object of scorn, exploitation, psychological and physical abuse—a sideshow freak whose ugliness people paid to see. His position was not unlike that of the sinful woman who bathed the feet of Jesus. He earned his living by that which was most ugly in him. The most touching scene occurs when Merrick tells his friend and doctor, Frederick Treves, that because of the doctor's kindness and caring, he learned to love himself. This is what Jesus did for Mary and what we need to do for each other. Personal prayer provides the opportunity to know that love of God for us which enables us to love ourselves despite our ugliness and to assume this forgiving stance, with Jesus, towards all we meet.

Many of us see only the interior grotesqueness and distortion of ourselves—the void within. We cry out in horror as the elephant man did when he first saw his image in a mirror. Like John Merrick and the sinful woman, we need others to mirror back to us the real beauty that is in us when the light of God's Son and his light in others shines in our darkness. Then we can forgive and love. Prayer is like that mirror, a loving look that cures, converts, creates.

To pray is to choose life, the life of God in Jesus Christ, which frees us to say yes to being uprooted and radicalized. Anyone who prays will gradually be changed. That is partially why prayer frightens us, for we somehow resist the change. But as we come in honesty before our God, not hiding even the ugliest and darkest side of our reality or our image of ourselves, we will become a new creation.

Repentance will be a constant dimension of our prayer. Conversion will flow from every hearing of the word, and we will see every dimension of life with the new eyes of faith. This uprooting will transform us into more human, whole, loving, and forgiving people—people who have become, in our new radical relationship with the Lord, truly life-giving, truly responsive to our sisters and our brothers.

Reconciliation as Prayer

Repent and believe the Good News.

Mark 1:15

The Good News is that God loves us. In order to relate the previous chapter to the sacrament of repentance, of "turning around" (reconciliation), let Fr. Carroll speak for a moment in the first person.

When I was seventeen and about to enter the seminary, I was a terribly spoiled young man. The entire summer before I left, I indulged myself in everything I was supposedly able to enjoy only this final time. As I rushed through this summer of final fling, I played golf daily, swam, water-skied, drank beer, and was rarely at home. One day, about three weeks before summer ended, my mother stopped me as I whirled from the house and said quietly, without accusation: "Pat, I love you. I'll miss you when you are gone, and I certainly haven't seen much of you all summer." She struck me right between the eyes. I knew my mother loved me, knew I loved her. I just had not thought about it very much. This was a conversion experience, a realization of something I knew but had been missing in my selfish, hectic pace. I had been ignoring her and my family. I *regretted* my blindness and stupidity. I was *ashamed* because I had not responded at all to the deepest and most powerful love in my life at the time. I was *sorry* in the face of love now recognized. The final three weeks of that summer were decidedly different from the previous ones. I had been cared for and cured by love remembered and renewed.

Whatever purgatory finally turns out to be, it must be an experience something like the above. We cannot imagine it as a place so much as an experience—the deep, final realization of sorrow at how deeply, consistently, faithfully, and foolishly we been loved by God and by others all through our lives, and how unfaithful, unaware, and unresponsive we have been. This will be a purging experience, indeed, the kind of radical, transforming experience that a mother's love can create here.

The prayer of solitude and the sacramental prayer of reconciliation seek to render Christian persons more deeply aware of that lasting love that waits for us to know it and be changed by it. In this chapter we consider the sacrament of reconciliation, not as a ritual action but as prayer. This prayer of radical transformation calls us out of sin into freedom and does not just fritter around the edges of our lives, making erasures off some internal, eternal blackboard. Some of the material of the previous chapter is interwoven here, for it all applies to sacramental as well as personal prayer.

We will not be concerned with the details of the rite of reconciliation, whether celebrated individually or communally. Rather, we hope to reach behind the rite and touch on the attitudes called forth by the Church in its renewal. Curiously, there is no change asked of the penitent within the new rite, but the minister is asked to celebrate within the context of Scripture and prayer and to be present as a healing sign of God's love rather than as judge. We are encouraged to carry on the healing dialogue in honesty, dealing not just with our actions but with our lives and our relationship with God and others, sometimes symbolized by particular actions. Everything about the sacrament is prayer: prayer involved with life, prayer that is a personal response to God, prayer that is radical in enabling God to get at the roots of our lives with his love. The sacrament invites us to let ourselves be turned around (repentant, converted) because we have recognized God's love.

Sin

Before we consider the sacrament, let us look again at sin, that reality in our lives which the sacrament specifically confronts. In order to comprehend this sacrament proclaiming that where sin abounds grace does more abound, we focus on the ways in which sin and love struggle for mastery in our lives.

Whatever else we say about sin, we must again begin with the realization that it is always an offense against love, a failure in a love relationship. Sin is not simply the breaking of a law totally outside myself. For the Jewish people, following their understanding of Hosea and the other prophets, sin was always "adultery"—infidelity within a relationship, the breaking of a covenant, a turning to other gods despite the deep love of Yahweh God for his people.

Sin is always a missing of the mark, an off-centeredness, a missing of the target we have established as our chosen goal. As we grow into adulthood, we develop a sense of what our lives are about, and we direct our lives towards certain goals and goods. We gradually center ourselves on God, however that God is named—The Good, Love, Ground of our Being. Sin bespeaks all the ways we wander from what we know and choose to be good for us.

Scripture and sin

For believers, the word of God, Scripture, helps us to know what is the mark and what, conversely, is deadly for us. In the seventeenth chapter of St. John's Gospel, we read how Jesus prays that we may be so completely one that the world can believe. Sin, then, is the failure to value, aim at, or in any way achieve that unity with others that is the infallible sign of our acceptance of God's love for us. This necessary Christian unity is expressed another way in the first letter to the Corinthians (12:12–26), where Paul concludes his marvelous analogy of the body-human compared with the body of Christ: "No part of the body can say to any other part of the body, I do not need you." Sin is saying in word or action to someone else: "I do not need you; you are not important to me." Sin, again, is a breakdown in a love relationship—a lack of appreciation for, or failure to achieve, the oneness invited by the Lord.

Because we are unable to accept the Lord's invitation to happiness, we are unhappy, unloving, joyless. In the fifth chapter of Matthew's Gospel, Jesus tells us where happiness lies. Happy are the poor, the peacemakers, the meek, those who hunger and thirst for justice, those who suffer persecution for the sake of the gospel. We are so often not truly happy as human beings because we are unable or unwilling to internalize the paradoxical values of Jesus. We realize that we do not achieve either this awareness or the ability to act on it by ourselves. We are loved into them. We do not make a decision and then on our own steam fulfill the dream of the beatitudes; we are assimilated into Jesus, who speaks them. The roots of our lives are gradually recreated until, in some measure at least, we live now not ourselves, but Christ lives in us.

Finally, in our cursory look at sin, we recall the judgment scene in the twenty-fifth chapter of Matthew. What we see is not a picture of what the final judgment will look like, not a script waiting to be played out, but rather the clearest New Testament statement about the criteria for that judgment. Matthew presents, on Jesus' lips, the criteria for evaluating our lives not only at the end but right now. We remove ourselves from the sight of God and from our own peace with ourselves right now if we ignore the hungry, the thirsty, the imprisoned, the homeless. Sin, then, is the inability to share in the compassion of God for those who are suffering among us and around us.

We could continue to speak at length about sin, but from the above it is clear that when we talk of reconciliation, we talk of turning back, repenting, being converted from what destroys our present and our ultimate happiness and fosters our alienation from others. We speak of a radical turn, in prayer, from various kinds of death to life.

Reconciliation: meaning of the word

Reconciliation, the prayer and sacrament of conversion, celebrates the possibility of beginning again. In Christ everything is restored, starts anew. We can always accept God's love and begin to love again.

In the past we have used other words, good words, to speak of the sacramental experience.

102

Most of us grew up hearing about the sacrament of penance. The word for penance comes from the Greek *metanoia,* the Latin *paenitentia,* meaning "repentance," "conversion," literally "turning around," "turning away," "starting over." Penance was literally, then, the sacrament of turning around and starting over, facing a loving God. Centuries went by, and language shifted, and the word *penance* took on a secondary and misleading connotation of discipline, hard work, or the action (penance) we performed to make up for our sins. Within the sacrament itself, the "penance" was prayers we said or, more rarely, something we did to satisfy for our sins. The truth, of course, is that we cannot satisfy for our sins. The Good News is that we do not have to; Jesus already has. So, though *penance* was at one time an adequately descriptive word for the experience of prayer we speak of, it has become inept.

We also spoke of receiving this sacrament as "going to confession." Again, the word *confession* is excellent, denoting an act of faith in or with others, a faith alongside a believing community. The word should and could mean an "act of trust," a "profession" of our belief in the loving mercy of God. But it has come to focus on what we said, the admission of our faults, our humble recitation of small and large sins. We spoke of confessing not our faith in God but our sins, placing the emphasis in precisely the wrong place—on ourselves. We focused on what we had done rather than on what God had done for us. We spoke less of placing our trust in the loving mercy of God than of accurately naming our failures. So what had been an excellent word, *confession,* also has become inept, inadequate.

Today the Church, in renewing the sacrament and inviting us to a deeper understanding of the liturgical act, speaks of the sacrament of reconciliation. *Reconciliation* indicates that they who have been estranged (separated, alienated) are again one, as they have been in the past and are intended to be. It denotes the reunion of lovers. We note the important fact that it is we who have turned away, we who have wandered and come back, not God. "Yahweh's love will last forever, his faithfulness till the end of time," and we have rediscovered it, reaccepted it, and been reconciled to it.

And we speak, finally, in this regard, not so much of receiving the sacrament as of celebrating it. We are not the passive recipients of God's love but the active respondents to it. It is not task or penance, but celebration.

Jesus saves

The sacrament of reconciliation does not save us. Renewed faith in Christ saves us, calling us back to community, back to him. The severed branch longs for the life of the vine. The prodigal daughter or son wakes up one morning and decides to return to the love of the Father and the celebration that is always waiting in the Father's house. Grace pre-

cedes the sacrament and then is confirmed, celebrated, and deepened in it. The son, wallowing in
the pigsty (and, as a Jewish boy, as unable to eat
the pigs as to eat the food the pigs eat—i.e., at the
very bottom), remembers what his father is really
like. This remembering is a grace-filled act. We
would never go to the Father, never celebrate this
sacrament, unless we already knew the forgiveness
available to us whenever we finally should come to
our senses. God's loving forgiveness is always
present; it is not created, caused, nor totally conditioned by the sacrament. The son already knew,
but his knowledge was confirmed when he met his
father again. His trust in the abundance of that sur-
prising love, which he celebrated with all his
father's friends, was deepened as the dead came to
life again, the lost was found, the alienated was
reconciled.

In the twenty-first chapter of John's Gospel, the
marvelous story of Jesus and Peter celebrating the
sacrament of reconciliation further establishes the
dimensions of this liturgical prayer. Peter has
recently denied any knowledge of Jesus, separating
himself from that loving friendship and letting his
friend be led to death. Now they meet at the
lakeside. The love of Jesus has still been present
overwhelmingly in the catching of fish and the
serving of a meal. Jesus takes Peter aside and asks,
"Do you love me?" We often read the story—
accurately, we suspect—as an opportunity for
Peter to thrice affirm what he had thrice denied:

105

his knowledge and love of Jesus. But beneath that truth one suspects a deep, personal, loving need of Jesus to know for sure that Peter also loves him. He wants to hear Peter say those words, affirm that reality, and be reunited with him, reconciled to him. Jesus' love, however, does not depend on Peter's answer. He has loved Peter first, has already forgiven him, and the scene allows Peter to celebrate and deepen what is already true.

It is not sufficient that Peter and Jesus are once again friends. We said in the last chapter that forgiveness precedes mission. Each affirmation of love is accompanied by a missioning to others, a sending forth: "Feed my sheep, . . . feed my sheep, . . . feed my little lambs." The God who loves us sends us. The God who forgives us calls us. Peter is not merely forgiven but also recommissioned in his role as leader of the new community gathered in the name of the forgiver. His post is not vacated because of his failures, not given to another who will be stronger and more faithful. The Lord's faith in Peter is not destroyed because of Peter's weakness. Precisely in the face of Peter's human frailty, the Lord again sends him to care for his people.

The penance within the sacrament of reconciliation is meant to be similar to this. It is not a prayer we say or an action we perform to make up for our sins. Rather, it is a step in the direction we want to go and where the Lord wants us to go, although we have failed in the past. We are recommissioned to God's people when we are reconciled with God. "As I have loved you, love one another." The radical conversion of the sacramental prayer—the realization that we have indeed turned around, have changed—is indicated and signified by the step we take in the direction we now begin.

The sacrament and life

The experience of this sacrament is not separate from the ebb and flow of our daily lives, apart from which it cannot be effective. Our reconciliation with God and our ability to accept this rediscovered love and this reconstituted commission come from our life-experiences: can we believe in forgiveness without having seen it, known it, felt it on a human level? This prayer also provides a key incentive to our ongoing human experience. If I have been forgiven, I in turn can forgive, need to forgive. The steward who has been relieved of a huge debt must relieve the smaller debts that others owe him. If this sacrament becomes real and effective (efficacious), it will weave itself ever more deeply into the fabric of the entire life of the community and individual.

We are often struck with the reality of Murray's discovery in *A Thousand Clowns*. He practices apologizing to his girlfriend by saying "Forgive me, I'm sorry," to numerous people on the streets of New York. He finds himself amazed that everyone accepts his apology. One woman even accepts it for herself and her dog: "I forgive you, and Poopsie forgives you." Everyone out there on the streets believes that someone somewhere owes them an apology. The need for forgiveness is pervasive, universal; so is the need to forgive. The sacrament, the prayer of forgiveness, reminds us of that fact, deepens it, celebrates it, and invites us to live always aware of it. The cycle is constant. We have been forgiven, we forgive . . . have been forgiven, forgive . . . have been forgiven, forgive.

Communal dimension of the sacrament

The familiar gospel story of Jesus curing the paralytic (Mark 2) serves as an example of the sacrament of reconciliation and healing. We are all paralyzed in one way or another. We are all unable to walk, love, and serve as we would like. Sin is often more aptly described by paralysis than by ill-will or viciousness.

The context of the story speaks of a crowd gathered around Jesus—believers and potential believers, people who trusted in (or would come to trust in) the healing power of Jesus. As he spoke to the crowd in the house, a clamor occurred outside. A paralyzed man is brought by friends who want him to experience this saving power. The man could not get there on his own, perhaps would not believe in the possibility of healing if left to his own discouragement and years of suffering. He needed those friends to bring him to the Lord. They carry him to the roof and lower him before the crowd, before the Lord. We, too, are brought by a community of one or many. The end of the story, "We have never seen anything like this . . .," indicates that the community not only promotes the healing but is enriched by it. Our faith is deepened as we perceive the healing power of Jesus alive in the limbs of another.

The sacrament of faith

The same Scripture passage offers a variety of other insights into the prayer of healing. What causes the growth and blossoming of reconciling faith? Initially, the man placed before Jesus asks for the obvious, superficial, definable healing of his limbs. Jesus says to him, "Be of good faith, your sins are forgiven." We imagine the man saying, "That's really nice, but it's about my legs!" How often we ask for one thing—the wrong thing— thinking the problem is in one place when it really is in another. We misidentify our *dis*-ease, and we come to know the deeper, real healing in our lives only by its visible, external signs.

How often, for example, someone speaks to a confessor, saying, "Forgive me, Father, I lied three times, I stole three times, I had four dirty thoughts." These petty failings seem disparate, isolated. Their healing could be simple, superficial. A few moments' discussion easily yields the reali-

109

zation that the woman speaking is struggling in the whole relationship with her quite distant husband. Because it is so difficult to talk with him, she has begun to lie, avoid the truth, mislead him. When she needs money, rather than try to work out the necessary explanation, she simply takes it without asking. In her longing for honest intimacy, she has begun to think romantically of other, kinder men. The healing that she seeks from God lies much deeper than the healing she came to seek consciously. She needs to be lifted up, empowered, and encouraged to begin again to try to speak and listen to her husband. The sacrament, as prayer, needs to reach beneath the surface to touch her in her deeper need.

And there are always skeptics everywhere, those who do not and will not believe. "Who is this man to forgive sins?" In every community there are always the curious, those who are there to watch, to wait, to judge, but not to be involved, not to receive or to give love. They undercut the faith of others, but they cannot kill it.

We look at the healing of the paralytic. You or I perhaps could have been there to hear the words, "Get up and walk," and been unable to believe them. "I do not know how." "I'm not one of your walkers." "I've never walked before, how can I now?"

But there is something in the voice of Jesus, something in his look, something in the entire charged atmosphere, that frees the man to believe that he can be cured, changed, healed, made into a new creation. The words and presence of Jesus are important, but so is the faith of the paralyzed man. Jesus could have spoken to him forever, but, until the man had the courage to put one of his toes on the ground and give it a try, he never would have been changed. He had to believe in the power of Jesus to effect the transformation, or the change would not have taken place. He could have turned his wheelchair into a throne and refused to be different than he had so far known himself to be. Then, like us so often, he could have left the confessional or reconciliation room exactly as he had entered—unchallenged and unchanged.

For the prayer of reconciliation to be a freeing prayer, a renewing prayer within the celebration of the sacrament, two things must happen. The words and deeds of Jesus need somehow to get through to us both individually and communally. We cannot perform empty, automatic ritual, saying words, making gestures with no heart, no spirit. Somehow Jesus needs to look at us and speak to us in a way that fosters faith.

Second, we need to believe that the Lord will do what he says he can do. We need to trust that the healing can take place, that we can be different. We need to try to walk in a new and unfamiliar but far more freeing and exciting way. How often in the past we have celebrated a sacrament, been told of our healing, but remained the same. Jesus was there, we were there, but no effective meeting took place. The challenge of the renewed sacrament, in its revised liturgical form, is to create the environment, the prayer, by which we can truly experience the saving, reconciling word of Christ and respond to that word in newfound faith. We do not have to be paralyzed in that old way any longer. We can walk, run, jump, and love as we never have before. Touched at the root of who we are or have known ourselves to be, we need never be the same again.

Reconciliation as vocation

Still, as in every sacrament, reconciliation is a vocation to be lived into and not an accomplished fact. We receive the invitation to become other. We are not usually totally new as we walk from the room of reconciliation, but we are certainly called and invited to become different, to grow into a new self-understanding, a new rootedness in the Lord. The individual and the community celebrating this sacrament are rarely fully completed and fully believing at the time of the celebration. We grow into a trust, try a new behavior, and encourage others to this new life which gradually takes root in us. The sacrament can sometimes work rather powerfully and carry an instantaneous effect, but usually we get up only gradually from our accustomed mats as that prayer gets to the core of our life and changes the way we see and do everything.

For the world

Briefly we relate all the above to what we said before: this sacrament, like every other sacrament, is not for us alone, not for the individual, not for the community that celebrates it. It exists for the entire Church and for the world. This community is called to witness to the possibility of forgiveness, of beginning again. The entire Church—the sacramental, reconciling Church—is called to extend a healing word to a badly wounded world. The reality of this sacramental reality in our Church lives must lead to a Christian presence in our world that witnesses to the ubiquitous healing presence of God.

Sacrament as a pervasive reality

The sacramental reality of reconciliation occurs not only "in the box" or reconciliation room. As we pointed out in the previous chapter, the fruit of all prayer is ultimately and always change, uprooting, rerooting. The sacrament focuses that change and heightens our awareness of it. Moreover, though we often forget it, the primary sacrament for the forgiveness of sins is (as the Council of Trent teaches) the Eucharist. In the regular celebration of the Eucharist, we hear the converting word of God, open our mouths and hearts to receive Jesus, and are changed by his living presence in us. The words of the celebration, from penance rite to Communion ("Lamb of God, you take away the sins of the world . . ."), remind us of this. To meet Jesus is always to be reconciled to God, always to be radically changed.

The sacrament of reconciliation is also a reality that pervades the entire lives of believers. Perhaps it is most obviously present in any truly successful marriage. Any couple struggling to be a sacramental sign of God's faithful love must continually forgive and begin again. And every act of forgiveness is a true presence of the forgiving God in our lives. Beyond that, every time anyone forgives, God forgives. We proclaim and realize that forgiveness. For those whose sins you forgive, they are forgiven; for those whose sins you retain, they are retained" (John 20:22–23). Jesus spoke these words as his Easter message of peace when he breathed the gift of the Spirit upon his followers. And the words are spoken to the Church, not just to priests. God is able to forgive and to get at changing the people he loves whenever we mediate that forgiveness. In a very real sense, God's ability to touch us, while not dependent on the sacrament, is indeed limited, inhibited, or helped by our forgiveness of one another.

We are all sinners. There are no other kinds of folks. We all fail to be everything we want to be. We are not sufficiently loving or adequately concerned with justice. We do not promote peace or foster friendship as we would like. We are con-

114

tinually falling short. Our image of God is not that of a tyrant with a thunderbolt in his hand, about to fire it upon us as he peers down in disgust, wondering, "When are they ever going to understand?" Rather, he looks with the eyes of compassion and love, thrilled about us as he reflects, "Wow, they are finally starting to catch on!" Still, we remain quite fallible sinners. The significant reality is that we are sinners, but always called, loved, chosen, and redeemed sinners. The deepest reality is that despite our sins, God loves us. And that realization is the foundation and root of our possibility to change, to be rerooted.

Prayer invites us constantly to be other than we are in the light of the love we have received. "Believe the Good News that God loves you!"

Conclusion:

Solitude to Sacrament

When Jesus heard [of the death of John the Baptizer], he withdrew by boat to a deserted place by himself. The crowds heard of it and followed him on foot from the towns. When he disembarked and saw the vast throng, his heart was moved with pity, and he cured their sick. As evening drew on, his disciples came to him with the suggestion: "This is a deserted place and it is already late. Dismiss the crowds so that they may go to the villages and buy some food for themselves." Jesus said to them: "There is no need for them to disperse. Give them something to eat yourselves." "We have nothing here," they replied, "but five loaves and a couple of fish." "Bring them here," he said. Then he ordered the crowds to sit down on the grass. He took the five loaves and two fish, looked up to heaven, blessed and broke them and gave the loaves to the disciples, who in turn gave them to the people. All those present ate their fill. The fragments remaining, when gathered up, filled twelve baskets. Those who ate were about five thousand, not counting women and children.

Matt 14:13–21

We have all experienced the death of a beloved relative or friend. Most of us who come from a deeply Christian tradition react to such a loss with two deep, faith-based needs. We need to separate ourselves for a moment from routine life and let the reality, the pain, and the hope sink in. We need to wrestle with our loss in the quiet of our hearts; we need that awful leisure Emily Dickinson speaks about as "our faith to regulate."

Later we need to come together with others who have known and loved our friend or ourselves and somehow capture in sign and symbol our shared hope that life does not end but merely changes. We need to sacramentalize our loss with others within a shared-faith context. We need both solitude and sacrament.

Death is not the only human event that necessitates this complimentarity. Somehow all of life needs to be internalized, related to our ultimate concerns, then brought with others into further consciousness. We do not live alone as islands; only in relationship to others are we able to discover anything about ourselves. As praying, growing persons trying to let God love us ever more fully into life, we need to pray alone and we need to pray with others. Solitude leads us not only to communal, sacramental prayer, but it leads us also to be sacramental persons in the lives of others. Sacramental prayer leads us more vigorously into life, but it also touches in us the need to be alone and quiet with our God. Solitude leads to sacrament; sacrament leads to solitude.

In the Gospel passage with which this chapter begins, Jesus has learned of the death of his friend John, a friend whose life and mission, while quite different from his own, could easily lead to the same fatal conclusion. In the context of Matthew's Gospel, this news of John's death in chapter fourteen comes as other parts of Jesus' ministry are being re-evaluated. He has begun—in chapter thirteen—to speak in the veiled language of parables, explaining them only to those closest to him. Later chapters will form the Book of the Church, that part of the Gospel geared particularly to his disciples who will pass on his message. But now, faced with John's death and his own uncertain mission, Jesus withdraws to the desert. He steps aside to ponder, to reflect with the Father on what it means and where to go. In solitude, he renews within himself his vision, his determination, his sense of being loved, his desire to love in return.

Then the crowds discover him, and he is moved from solitude to community, to service, to being sacrament. It is no accident that the Book of the Church in Matthew (13:53—18:35) begins with the sacrament of the Church, a miracle steeped in the language and symbolism of the Eucharist, the essential bread of the life of the Church. Jesus, out of his own solitude and withdrawal, moves back into interaction with the crowds and eventually celebrates with them the new "manna" of the desert, the new covenant sign of God's continued nourishing presence to his people. No assertion is made by Matthew or ourselves that this feeding was the sacrament of the Eucharist in the strictest sense. But the story is told in language reminding the early community and us of that enduring mystery (he took, he blessed, he broke, he gave).

Jesus moves from solitude to sacrament.

Moreover, Jesus challenges the disciples to give the people something to eat themselves. He invites them to rely on their own resources to care for the people. They can't, they are paralyzed. They need to rely on Jesus for the power to serve, feed, and care for the crowds. In union with the people, they can take their very little bit and make it more than enough for all.

This familiar, symbol-laden passage seems an apt one on which to center our concluding remarks. Throughout this book we have tried to show (1) how prayer leads to life, and sacraments are prayer; (2) how prayer invites and demands response, and sacraments are prayer; (3) how prayer gets at the roots of our lives and empowers us to be more alive and more responsive than we have been, and sacraments are prayer. In solitude and together in sacrament, we meet our God. From solitude and sacrament we go to nourish others.

At the outset of this book we asked how we could remember, deepen, trust, and make operative our experiences of God. We have shown what these experiences might lead to, how they might affect us, and how the interrelationships of private and communal prayer both foster and support these experiences.

Deep in every human being lies the sense of loneliness and incompleteness, the awareness that alone I am not enough. Out of that loneliness I am tempted to look for that other one, that perfect relationship, that totally fulfilling love that satisfies my every need. I perhaps tightly grab hold of someone or something, experiencing initial joy, then frustration and finally despair. No one, no thing, can totally fulfill me. I become like a hand tightly joined to another, unable to move freely and function as a hand while inextricably bound.

As we grow in wisdom, age, and grace, we learn that what we desperately need is to discover God—alive, personal, and loving us—somewhere in the depths of our hearts. In the discovery, we become more whole, and we move towards others who have also met that God—the God in us discovers the God in them—our hands touch, steeple-like, and we form church. We are not church when we come together as people who do not pray alone, who try to draw and sustain our total life of faith out of a community of semi-believers. We are not church when we remain alone, sucking our religious thumbs in isolation with our private God. We are church when together we find God in solitude and sacrament, out of which we become sacrament to the world. We mirror the compassion

121

of God as we continue the sacramental ministry of Jesus.

In solitude we have been made aware of our deeply bonded unity with God, who is father and mother to us. We have celebrated that union within some community of faith. We are able to move into our world as people who welcome everyone into our families, societies, hearts, lives.

In solitude this initial realization that we are daughters and sons of God has been confirmed over and over again, leading us to be not just receivers of God's love but bringers of God's Spirit to our world. We have celebrated this confirmation with others who share such convictions and dreams. We have become part of a people that strengthens the sense of giftedness of all we meet. At least we try to reinforce that specialness that is some part of everyone.

In solitude we have experienced in profound ways our union with the Lord Jesus and our communion with all because of him. We have celebrated this in sign and sacrament over and over again. We have said with lips and lives that such union of all is possible and worth every struggle to achieve.

In solitude we have known God's love when we have failed, and we have felt the forgiving touch of friends and enemies alike. We have celebrated the never-ending possibility of beginning once again, getting off our mats and learning how to walk in brand new ways. And we have brought that mending, healing love into our lives.

In moments of ministry, of marriage, or of death, we have likewise been touched in one way or another, alone and with our Church. We have known God's service, the service of others, and our own, and we have celebrated that together. We have seen fidelity and constant love through time, through pain, till death. And somehow we have seen even death as victory and not the end.

We can imagine no better way to end our reflections on solitude and sacrament than with verses 10–21 from Psalm 145. They enflesh our continued prayer as we deepen our awareness of our God, our celebration of that splendid gift, and our commitment to the service of his people.

> *Let all your works give you thanks, O LORD,*
> *and let your faithful ones bless you.*
> *Let them discourse of the glory of your*
> *kingdom*
> *and speak of your might,*
> *Making known to [all] your might*
> *and the glorious splendor of your*
> *kingdom. . . .*
> *The LORD is faithful in all his words*
> *and holy in all his works.*
> *The LORD lifts up all who are falling*
> *and raises up all who are bowed down.*
> *The eyes of all look hopefully to you,*
> *and you give them their food in due*
> *season;*

123

You open your hand
and satisfy the desire of every living
thing. . . .
The LORD is near to all who call upon him,
to all who call upon him in truth.
He fulfills the desire of those who fear him,
he hears their cry and saves them. . . .
May my mouth speak the praise of the LORD,
and may all flesh bless his holy name
forever and ever.

SUGGESTED READING

Abhishiktananda. *Prayer*. Philadelphia: Westminster, 1973.

Baily, Raymond. *Thomas Merton on Mysticism*. New York: Doubleday, 1975.

Bloom, Anthony. *Beginning to Pray*. New York: Paulist, 1971.

Burrows, Ruth. *Guidelines for Mystical Prayer*. Denville, N.J.: Dimension, 1980.

Callahan, William, S.J., and Cardman, Francine. *The Wind is Rising*. Washington, D.C.: Quixote Center, 1978.

Carroll, L. Patrick, S.J. *To Love, To Share, To Serve: Challenges to a Religious*. Collegeville, Minn.: The Liturgical Press, 1979.

Carroll, L. Patrick, S.J., and Dyckman, Katherine Marie, S.N.J.M. *Inviting the Mystic, Supporting the Prophet*. New York: Paulist, 1981.

Caulfield, Sean, O.C.S.O. *The Experience of Praying*. New York: Paulist, 1980.

De Mello, Anthony, S.J. *Sadhana: A Way to God, Christian Exercises in Eastern Form*. St. Louis: Institute of Jesuit Sources, 1979.

Dunne, Tad, S.J. *We Cannot Find Words*. Denville, N.J.: Dimension, 1981.

Farrell, Edward. *Prayer Is a Hunger*. Denville, N.J.: Dimension, 1972.

Finley, James. *Merton's Place of Nowhere.* Notre Dame: Ave Maria, 1978.

Fowler, James W. *Stages of Faith.* San Francisco: Harper & Row, 1981.

Fox, Matthew, O.P. *On Becoming a Musical, Mystical Bear: Spirituality American Style.* New York: Paulist, 1976.

———. *A Spirituality Named Compassion.* Minneapolis: Winston, 1979.

Green, Thomas. *When the Well Runs Dry: Prayer Beyond the Beginnings.* Notre Dame: Ave Maria, 1979.

Hocken, Peter. *Prayer, Gift of Life.* New York: Paulist, 1974.

Johnston, William, S.J. *The Inner Eye of Love.* San Francisco: Harper & Row, 1978.

———. *The Mirror Mind.* San Francisco: Harper & Row, 1981.

———. *Silent Music: The Science of Meditation.* New York: Harper & Row, 1979.

Jung, Carl G. *Man and His Symbols.* New York: Doubleday, 1964.

———. *Psyche and Symbol: A Selection from the Writings of C. G. Jung,* ed. Violet S. de Laszlo. New York: Doubleday, 1958.

Kelsey, Morton. *Caring.* New York: Paulist, 1981.

———. *The Other Side of Silence: A Guide to Christian Meditation.* New York: Paulist, 1976.

———. *Transcend: A Guide to the Spiritual Quest.* New York: Crossroad, 1981.

Leech, Kenneth. *True Prayer.* London: Sheldon, 1980.

McNamara, William, O.C.D. *Mystical Passion: Spirituality for a Bored Society*. New York: Paulist, 1977.

Main, John, O.S.B. *Word into Silence*. New York: Paulist, 1980.

Maloney, George, S.J. *The Breath of the Mystic*. Denville, N.J.: Dimension, 1974.

———. *Inward Stillness*. Denville, N.J.: Dimension, 1976.

Merton, Thomas. *New Seeds of Contemplation*. 2nd ed. rev. New York: New Directions, 1972.

———. *Contemplation in a World of Action*. New York: Doubleday, 1973.

Nouwen, Henri. *Clowning in Rome: Reflections on Solitude, Celibacy, Prayer and Contemplation*. New York: Doubleday, 1979.

———. *Reaching Out: The Three Movements of the Spiritual Life*. New York: Doubleday, 1975.

———. *The Way of the Heart*. New York: Seabury, 1981.

———. *The Wounded Healer: Ministry in Contemporary Society*. New York: Doubleday, 1972.

Pennington, M. Basil, O.C.S.O. *The Centering Prayer: Renewing an Ancient Christian Prayer Form*. New York: Doubleday, 1980.

———. *Daily We Touch Him: Practical Religious Experiences*. New York: Doubleday, 1979.

Powers, Joseph, S.J. *Spirit and Sacrament*. New York: Seabury, 1973.

Sanford, John. *Healing and Wholeness*. New York: Paulist, 1977.

———. *The Kingdom Within*. New York: Paulist, 1980.

———. *The Man Who Wrestled with God.* New York: Paulist, 1981.

Segundo, Juan, S.J. *The Sacraments Today,* trans. John Drury. Theology for Artisans of a New Humanity Series, vol. 4. New York: Orbis, 1974.

Topel, John, S.J. *The Way to Peace: Liberation Through the Bible.* New York: Orbis, 1979.

Whitehead, Evelyn E., and Whitehead, James D. *Christian Life Patterns: The Psychological Challenges and Religious Invitations of Adult Life.* New York: Doubleday, 1979.